A Rite on the Edge

A Rite on the Edge

*The Language of Baptism and Christening
in the Church of England*

Sarah Lawrence

scm press

Published in 2019 by SCM Press
Editorial office
3rd Floor, Invicta House,
108–114 Golden Lane,
London EC1Y 0TG, UK
www.scmpress.co.uk

SCM Press is an imprint of Hymns Ancient & Modern Ltd
(a registered charity)

Hymns Ancient & Modern® is a registered trademark of
Hymns Ancient & Modern Ltd
13A Hellesdon Park Road, Norwich,
Norfolk NR6 5DR, UK

British Library Cataloguing in Publication data

A catalogue record for this book is available
from the British Library

978-0-334-05850-2

Typeset by Regent Typesetting
Printed and bound by
CPI Group (UK) Ltd

Contents

List of figures

Foreword

How I wish this fascinating, lucid book had been available 40 years ago when I started work as an assistant curate in the Church of England. In those days, I conducted what I would have called 'baptismal visits' with parents seeking what they would have called 'christening' for their children. A product of the rationalist liberal modernist world view that produced Vatican 2, the New English Bible and the Alternative Service Book, I believed that a combination of passionate commitment to a distinctive post-Christendom Church and cognitive clarity about Christian discipleship should enlighten and convert 'nominal' Christians seeking christening for their children (apparently as a matter of unthinking vestigial habit) into keen church members actively living out their public faith promises as baptized members of the community.

Imagine my disappointment when, having appeared to have signed on the dotted line with informed consent to all this before the day, most of the families of baptized infants never appeared within the church doors again after the ceremony itself. In my darker moments, I felt used and disappointed. Why had these nice, decent people who seemed honest and truthful made important promises that they did not intend to keep? Were they just social conformists seeking a kind of magical supernatural under-seal for their infants, or wanting an excuse for a family party? Or, worse, had I myself failed to explain properly the nature and purpose of baptism so that it was actually my fault that they did not commit and join in?

Had I been lucky enough to have read Sarah Lawrence's book at that time, I would have been less perplexed at the apparent mutual incomprehension between clergy and parents over baptism/christening. More importantly, I would have been less hard on them and on myself.

A Rite on the Edge reveals that I and the families I was dealing with were heirs of long traditions of two very different – but valid – understandings of baptism/christening in England. On the one hand, clergy have, over many centuries, tended to focus on baptism as a cognitively understood act of commitment and initiation into serious personal sacrifice, service, even suffering and death. In some ways, it has been understood as a conscious standing outside wider society. On the other, many lay people have sought christening for a variety of motives including welcoming children into the world, naming them, providing them with adults who care for them, even making marriage-like vows to them, and bringing them into wider relations with the surrounding community, which *de facto* down the centuries was Christian in a country with an established Church. While ordinary people have emphasized the emotional, social, celebratory aspects of baptism/christening, clergy have been sceptical of these motives and understandings, stressing the disciplinary and intellectual aspects of the rite; some clergy have even manifested visceral disgust at the word 'christening' itself. The consequence has been a tragic stand-off. People have sought baptism/christening only to be discouraged, even rejected, by the pastors and communities who spend much of their time lamenting the marginalization and depletion of the Church.

According to Sarah Lawrence, what is required is that the rite should be understood in a holistic way that respects the warmth, inclusivity and emotionality of the lay understandings – while not forgetting the potential seriousness, intellectual commitment and demands of explicit Christian commitment embodied in clerical understandings. Sarah writes, '*Baptism* without *christening* becomes stale and cold, a harsh creed which commands doctrinal correctness but forgets human love. *Christening* without *baptism* becomes shallow and detached from the source of its meaning and significance.' Serious Christian commitment and having a party are not, then, necessarily mutually exclusive – that is good news, even gospel!

Sarah arrives at this humane, judicious position on the basis of novel and thorough research into the use of the words 'baptism' and 'christen' over time. The use of methods from corpus linguistics allows her – and her readers – to follow a long linguistic journey down the centuries through places like the law courts and the House of Lords so that we can better understand how the words 'christening'/'baptism' have been used and what their connotations are. Sarah wears her learning lightly and presents her findings clearly. But readers should be under no illusion that this is a pioneering, important piece of practical theology which is extremely well evidenced. Thus it is a vital, vivifying resource for pastoral practice and imagination. Furthermore, it contains not a single boring word – a tribute to her real desire to communicate with readers and make a difference in an important area where Church meets world.

I have often noticed that the more commonplace something is in life, the less likely it is that someone in theology will give it any attention. It is only very recently that the Church of England has begun to critically evaluate its own part in self-marginalizing into an exclusive sectarian rather than inclusive, societal position in the life of the nation. Sarah Lawrence's study will hasten this re-consideration, raising as it does important questions about who should be regarded as insiders and outsiders, who has the power to define the boundaries and nature of the Church, and how doctrine and liturgy should be constructed and performed at national and local levels. There are huge challenges here as the established Church, despite its rhetoric of good intentions with regard to inclusivity, continues to decline and lose the good will of those who had previously thought that this institution has a lot to do with them – even if they did not actively attend. Alongside readers in practical theology around the world, *A Rite on the Edge* should be read by every Church of England bishop, parish priest and ordinand, as well as by many lay people and the members of the doctrinal and liturgical committees of this and other churches. Whoever its readers are, they will not fail to be encouraged, educated, intrigued and, indeed, entertained. I very much hope that this will be the first of many brilliant books from Sarah Lawrence's most eloquent pen. I enthusiastically welcome it, hoping that everyone who reads it will get as much enlightenment and pleasure from it as I have.

Stephen Pattison
Sometime of University of Birmingham, UK

Introduction

As I began my ordained ministry in the Church of England over ten years ago, I was struck by the very different way that clergy and church-goers spoke about baptism, compared with non-churchgoing families who requested the rite for their children. Many clergy and congregation members saw these families as not being serious about the commitments they were making; they thought they did not understand the baptismal promises and/or did not mean to keep them. They often perceived them as being disrespectful of the church during the service itself, and were seen as abusing the rite, when they really wanted 'just a naming ceremony' or 'an excuse for a party'. When I visited families, however, they seemed to me to be very serious about what they were doing. They often could not articulate the reasons why, and the reasons they did give were not very 'religious', but they expressed a very deep belief that this was somehow the right thing to do. They perceived the Church as being 'their' church, and in some ways as key to their identity as a family. They wanted their child also to have this sense of belonging to the Church and have God bless him or her.

These families came and asked the Church for a *christening*; the Church offered them a *baptism*. I began to wonder whether this was more than just a difference in language. Does it reflect a deeper difference in under-standing what this rite is all about, and indeed what it means to be a Christian? I wondered whether an exploration of the different ways of speaking about baptism, between these two groups, might help clergy and churchgoers to understand better those families seeking occasional offices. I wondered whether, by beginning from a point of understanding and respect for the views of such families, the Church's ministry to them in response to their request for a christening might become more likely to open up doors to a greater exploration of faith, rather than put them off by misunderstanding and suspecting their motives. As I began to ask these questions and to delve deeper into what was going on with baptism in England, I found myself repeatedly coming back to the difference between these two words: *baptism* and *christening*. They seemed to act as a fault line which divided people into different religious groups who did not understand one another, who effectively spoke a different language when it came to baptism. I wanted to find out whether my impressions were representative of wider patterns in English culture and religion and, if so, what the churches can do to respond to these differences.

When I started to talk to people about the research I was carrying out – that I was interested in the differences between the words *baptism* and *christening* – the responses I received were often quite striking. Those who didn't go to church, and some of the less theologically engaged churchgoers, often looked embarrassed that they didn't understand the difference, and felt perhaps they were missing something. Many found the word *baptism* vaguely uncomfortable in some way they couldn't quite put their finger on; it was perhaps rather posh, perhaps excessively formal or religious sounding. It was the kind of technical word they often avoided using for fear of looking ignorant when they used it wrongly.

Clergy and committed churchgoers, however, sometimes had a remarkably visceral response to the word *christening*. One fairly senior clergyman remarked to me that it was a 'disgusting word'. Another argued that while 'baptism is a valid liturgical term, christening is at best an indication of poor understanding of the rite, at worst indicative of folk religion and superstition'. This sense that *baptism* is the 'right' term for the rite of Christian initiation, and *christening* is just the 'unofficial title'[1] was very common.

This book explores this problem by considering how the words *baptism* and *christening* have been used in ordinary British English discourse. It is based on research that explored language in letters, books, tracts, news-papers, court transcripts, conversations, sermons, social media messages and other examples of naturally occurring language over the course of over 500 years. It is offered as an insight into how non-churchgoers see baptism, and explores whether these perspectives can be helpful as a starting point for the Church to begin to teach about the faith, or whether they are antithetical to Christianity and should be seen as obstacles to true understanding that need to be cleared away before baptismal prepar-ation can begin. It is not a book about the Christian theology of baptism, which has been amply and ably explored in countless texts over the two millennia of the Church's history. Many of the perspectives explored here are very different to an orthodox Christian theology of baptism. In advocating taking them seriously, I am not disregarding the Christian heritage of teaching about this dominical sacrament. I do not argue that we should change our theology of baptism from the deep heritage of the tradition by replacing it with a thin veneer of popularism. However, I do argue that the meanings of baptism found in popular ways of speaking about this rite are worthy of being taken seriously, and represent a valid starting point from which clergy and committed churchgoers can begin to help families seeking a christening to explore the riches of the faith. At heart this book is aiming to be an aid to mission, to help Christians to make sense of what families seeking a baptism really want (even if on deeper exploration what they really want is perhaps a naming ceremony rather than baptism itself). It suggests a way of connecting with such families and helping them to begin the 'amazing journey' of faith that can begin with a christening.[2]

The book is concerned with the relationship between the people of England and their established Church. Some of the findings will be relevant in other parts of the UK, but others are specific to England. Similarly, some of the ideas here will be relevant to other denominations in the UK, and others will not. The focus on the English language means that English-speaking Christians in other parts of the world will find resonances and differences with what they read here. This may provide food for thought, and encourage those in churches in other settings to ask questions of their contexts, and especially about the differences in language and perspectives inside and outside the churches in their own cultures.

The book begins in Chapters 1 and 2 by exploring the problem. Chapter 1 asks why this division in the language used to talk about this rite opened up, and whether it is significant for pastoral practice for the churches in England today. Chapter 2 argues that the words *baptism* and *christening* have very different 'feels' and are used in different ways in British English, and asks what these differences might mean for a theology of christening in the Church of England today. It explores the importance of language in theology, in the Church and in society, and argues for a new methodological approach in practical theology, using linguistic research methods.

Chapter 3 gives an outline of how the language of *baptism* and *christening* has changed over the course of the English language. It argues that the different origins of these two words have affected their prestige over the centuries, and caused a social and religious split in how they were used from the sixteenth century onwards, becoming particularly entrenched in the eighteenth century and persisting up to the present day.

Chapters 4–7 explore themes that arise from non-churchgoers' use of language, especially the word *christening*. Chapter 4 looks at the significance of naming in popular understandings of this rite and asks whether it is theologically valid to see naming as a purely secular matter. Chapter 5 examines a new theme, which arose in connection with the word *christening* in the texts studied from the 1990s onwards, that of seeing baptism as an opportunity to make marriage-like vows of love and commitment towards the children. Chapter 6 considers the importance of godparents to non-churchgoing families and why godparents are much more strongly linked with *christening* than *baptism*, and what the implications of this may be for Church practice.

Chapters 7–9 then examine some of the concerns that clergy and committed churchgoers may have over the uses that non-churchgoers make of the rite of baptism. Chapter 7 examines the oft-heard concern that a christening, for such families, is 'just an excuse for a party'. Chapter 8 then asks whether the kind of baptism associated with the word *christening* and valued by non-churchgoing families is really the same thing as Christian baptism, whether what families seek would be more appropriately provided for by a non-religious ceremony, and whether it devalues this dominical sacrament of the Church to use it for such secular purposes. Chapter 9 asks whether it is appropriate for the understanding of a sacrament to be altered by those whom many in the Church do not see as true members, because they are not regular churchgoers or regular contributors to the life of the Church. Is the Church something that 'outsiders' can have a stake in? Or does it really not make sense to use the language of 'insiders' and 'outsiders' in a Church founded by the God who gave his only Son out of love for the whole world?

Chapter 10 concludes the book with some practical advice based on these findings, asking how churches can begin to properly value what is important to non-churchgoers in its understanding of this rite. We will see that, by understanding what is important to those who are not committed churchgoers, and re-embracing the ideas associated with the word *christening* as a Church, we can both learn and grow in our own theology of baptism and our ecclesiology, and build bridges to share the deep resources of our faith with those who are instinctively sympathetic to the Christian faith.

A note about terminology

In my doctoral thesis I studiously avoided the use of the words *baptism* or *christening* throughout, instead using the neutral term CI (Christian initiation) in order to avoid bias in using one or other of the words being studied. I have kept this terminology on the graphs and charts in this book as it would otherwise be confusing to distinguish the concept of Christian initiation from the words used to refer to it. However, this often made the language sound awkward and stilted, so I will not attempt this level of neutrality here and will use *baptism* and *christening* interchangeably. But it is important to note that one term is not 'right' and the other 'wrong', that both words have a pedigree of use in the English language, both have historical 'baggage'. One or other of these words feels more natural in some contexts than others: a 'christening dress' or a 'baptismal certificate', for example. However, the aim of this book is to problematize the language of baptism and christening and to ask what the origins and foundations are of the strong feelings that English speakers have about these words, to uncover the taken-for-granted and better understand what lies behind the words.

I am ordained in the Church of England and, like most committed churchgoers and theologically trained clergy, I find *baptism* a much more natural and comfortable word to use in most circumstances than *christening*. However, in order to maintain a neutrality in discussing these words, I will endeavour to use both terms. It is part of the aim of this book to make readers more aware of the language they use and the assumptions they make about people who use different language from them.

When referring to the research on which this book is based, I use *baptism* to refer to all 'bapt- words' (*baptism, baptized, baptizing, baptize, baptismal*, etc.) and *christening* to refer to all 'christen- words' (*christening, christened, christen*, etc.) unless stated otherwise. Where these terms are in italics, that is to indicate that I refer to the words *baptism* or *christening*, rather than to the concepts.

Notes

1 Grimes, R. L. (2000), *Deeply into the Bone: Re-inventing Rites of Passage*, Berkeley: University of California Press, p. 54.
2 Millar, S. (2018), *Life Events: Mission and Ministry at Baptisms, Weddings and Funerals*, London: Church House Publishing, ch. 2.

The problem of 'baptism' and 'christening'

As an Anglican priest, I have often instinctively felt that infrequent churchgoers prefer the word *christening*, while I and most churchgoers and clergy I know find the word uncomfortable, and are more likely to use *baptism*. This difference in language has occasionally been noted,[1] but little exploration has been done academically into whether this anecdotal impression of word preference can be empirically demonstrated and, if so, how the two terms are used by different groups within the community. I have wondered why and how the different terms arose, and whether the split in language reflects a cultural division between churchgoers and the wider society in England today. The Church of England has issued guidance on the different language on its website, which states:

> There is no difference between a christening service and a baptism service ... Babies are baptized during a christening service just as couples are 'married' during a wedding service.[2]

This approach is a step forward in helping both clergy to feel more comfortable using the word *christening* and parents to feel less alienated from the word *baptism*. It smooths over a conflict and seems a helpful pastoral way forward, and one that I now use in my parish setting. However, in terms of understanding the difference in language historically, and as a practical theologian understanding the social implications of these words, it conceals a conflict that needs to be understood better.

The baptism of infants from families who do not come to church has become a source of anxiety for many clergy, an embarrassment at what feels like a lie, or a distraction from the real business of communing with committed disciples of Christ who attend church. The fact that a family uses the word *christening* when they make their request usually indicates to the vicar that they are not regular churchgoers, probably have no intention of becoming churchgoers, and are being less than honest in undergoing a ceremony of acceptance into a Church that they do not intend the child to become a real part of. Thus, a tension often exists within this exchange, which families may feel but not really understand, as noted by Hill in her doctoral research into baptism families: 'From the parental perspective, seeking baptism in a largely secular age appears to them to be a virtuous request, so they cannot understand why some clergy appear dismissive.'[3] People who seek to have their children christened are asking to align themselves to the Church in an age in which this is not expected. The Church can easily, and usually unintentionally, offend and turn away those people who are most positive about it by the attitudes of clergy and churchgoers.

From the point of view of some clergy and regular churchgoers, however, this encounter feels very different. In the latter half of the twentieth century there was a growing sense of outrage at 'unchurched families who seek baptism for their children without any apparent interest in other aspects of the faith', as if the Church is 'acting as a retail outlet obliged by law to sell its goods to any who come'.[4] The request for baptism appears, to some clergy, perhaps especially those at the evangelical end of the spectrum, as being meaningless to families: 'many young parents, especially if they have had but rare contact with the church, will still want baptism in an automatic, individualistic, and uncommitting kind of way'.[5] This has led to particular tensions over what membership of the Church of England means, as its historic formularies, such as the Book of Common Prayer and Canon Law, require that all children duly presented must be baptized, and should not be delayed save for appropriate preparation.[6] The Church of England website states that this is still the case:

> The Church of England welcomes all babies, children and families –
> whatever shape that family takes ... You do not have to be an active
> churchgoer – as parents, you do not even have to have been christened
> yourselves. Everyone is welcome at their local church.[7]

Many clergy and churchgoers long to be welcoming to families, and see baptism ministry as a key way of connecting with those outside the Church: 'There is ... a recognition among clergy that [baptisms] offer an important pastoral opportunity.'[8] Yet even as the congregation says 'we welcome you' to the newly baptized in the service, the family is often marked out as different by their dress, their unease in the church setting, their unfamiliarity with the liturgy and expected forms of behaviour during a service, and by the fact that they usually stay in their seats while communion is administered. The words say that they belong, but the attitude of the clergy and regular churchgoers, and perhaps also their own feelings, tell them that they do not.

Baptism is very much a sacrament on the boundaries of the Church, a rite on the edge. It is essential to Christian identity, and is usually (although not always) seen as the way into the Church. Baptists and various Nonconformist denominations, while giving baptism a place of great importance, see it as a response to conversion, but it is conversion that makes a person a Christian, rather than baptism itself. The Catholic Church and the established Protestant denominations such as Lutheranism and Anglicanism (at least in their official formularies), however, see baptism as the marker of identity: what makes a person a Christian or not, a member of the Church or not. This is reflected in the Thirty-Nine Articles, number 27 of which states:

> Baptism is not only a sign of profession, and a mark of difference, whereby Christian men are discerned from others that be not christened, but it is also a sign of Regeneration or new Birth, whereby, as by an instrument, they that receive Baptism rightly are grafted into the Church.[9]

Despite this, many churchgoing Anglicans would not see those who are baptized, but do not attend church or fulfil certain other criteria such as having accepted a particular understanding of the gospel message, as being true Christians. They often find it difficult to understand why someone who has no interest in churchgoing or orthodox Christian commitment should seek to put their children through a ceremony in which they make promises they have no intention of keeping. It appears that baptism 'means nothing to them, they are not churchgoers'.[10] Many clergy are caught between the expectations of families seeking a christening, a desire to be welcoming to them, and a sense that they are 'casting their pearls before swine' (Matthew 7.6), allowing people to use a sacred rite as a mere excuse for a family party.

> On the positive side, [baptism] represents a unique opportunity for mission and evangelism, and roots the clergy firmly in the community. On the negative side, it can lead to a sense of being used and abused, so that much time and effort is spent on dealing with people who may have little genuine religious motivation at all.[11]

The positioning of baptism on the boundaries of church life can be seen by some as a threat to the Church, as those who seemingly have little interest in the Christian faith are, at least nominally, included as Christians. This threat is especially perceived by those who tend towards the congregational or sectarian end of the ecclesiological scale.[12] From a societal view of the Church, however, this very same factor of exposure of the Church to outsiders can be seen as an enriching opportunity for the Church.

Baptism is unique because it is a completely necessary and orthodox sacrament that is the mark of Christian identity, but alternately it also forces Christendom to be open to alterity and the diversity of texts, cultures, and bodies.[13]

This openness to outside voices, however, is not something that the Church has historically been very good at, and even some very liberal Christians may find it uncomfortable and difficult to do in practice. There are some within the Church who wish to be more generous in their interpretations of the motivations of parents, and perceive in parents a genuine seeking after God and desire to connect their child with the grace of God, even if they do not come to church. And yet even these ignore the word that families use when they seek a christening, and unconsciously correct them to the 'right' term, *baptism*. For example, Stephen Kuhrt says that he became convinced over time that most families genuinely wanted to respond to God when they were 'seeking a "christening"'.[14] Despite seeking to understand their points of view, Kuhrt found he could not use the word *christening* without using scare quotes. Similarly, Gillian Hill interviewed families about their experiences of requesting baptism for their children, and seeks to understand their point of view. But she, too, finds it almost impossible to use the word *christening*. A search of her thesis reveals that the word *christening* appears in the words of her interviewees, but she only uses it herself twice: once when talking about a christening robe, and another time in scare quotes.[15] If clergy cannot even acknowledge the words that such families use when they ask for a *christening*, how can we really understand what it means to them and why they ask? But does a difference in words really reflect any deeper difference in understanding? This will be the topic of the next chapter.

Notes

1 Carr, W. (1985), *Brief Encounters: Pastoral Ministry through the Occasional Offices*, London: SPCK, p. 66.

2 Church of England (2019), 'Is a "baptism" different to a "christening"?' Retrieved 4.7.19, from https://churchofenglandchristenings.org/for-parents/is-a-baptism-different-to-a-christening/.

3 Hill, G. (2006), 'Birthright or Misconception? An Investigation of the Pastoral Care of Parents in Relation to Baptismal Enquiries in the Church of England', PhD thesis, University of Portsmouth, p. 291.

4 Church of England (1995), *On the Way: Towards an Integrated Approach to Christian Initiation*, London: Church House Publishing, sections 5.18 and 5.19, p. 83.

5 Buchanan, C. (1992), *Infant Baptism in the Church of England: A Guide to the Official Position of the Church in its Formularies*, Nottingham: Grove Books, p. 15.

6 Church of England (2016), *Canons of the Church of England*, 7th edn. Retrieved 4.7.19, from www.churchofengland.org/more/policy-and-thinking/canons-church-england/section-b, canon B22.

7 This text was on the Church of England website in 2016, but has since been removed. It is still available here: Diocese of Rochester (2015), 'Top 10 Facts about Christenings'. Retrieved 4.7.19, from www.rochester.anglican.org/communications/news-in-brief/top-10-facts-about-christenings.php.

8 Liturgical Commission (2014), *Christian Initiation: Additional Texts in Accessible Language*. Retrieved 8.05.14, from www.churchofengland.org/media/1903641/baptism%20pack%20for%20trial%20use.pdf, p. 1. This is no longer available online.

9 Church of England (1662), *The Book of Common Prayer and the Administration of the Sacraments According to the Use of the Church of England*, standard edn, Cambridge: Cambridge University Press, pp. 622, 623.

10 Billings, A. (2004), *Secular Lives, Sacred Hearts: The Role of the Church in a Time of No Religion*, London: SPCK, p. 44.

11 Village, A. and L. J. Francis (2009), *The Mind of the Anglican Clergy: Assessing Attitudes and Beliefs in the Church of England*, Lewiston: Edwin Mellen Press, p. 57.

12 This is using the church–sect theory, devised by Weber and used by many sociologists of religion since. See Swatos Jr, W. H. (1998), 'Church–Sect Theory', in *Encyclopedia of Religion and Society*, ed. W. H. Swatos, W. H. Swatos, Jr and P. Kivisto, Walnut Creek, CA: AltaMira Press, pp. 90–3. In this book, I usually use the language of Linda Woodhead of 'societal churches' for the church-type model at one end of the scale, and 'sectarian' or 'congregational' to refer to the sect-type churches at the other end. See Woodhead, L. (2015), 'The Challenges that the New C of E Reports Duck', *Church Times*, 23.1.15, pp. 14–15.

13 Maslanka, C. W. (2012), 'Christening Women, Men, and Monsters: Images of Baptism in Middle English Hagiography and Romance', PhD thesis, University of Wisconsin-Madison, p. 272.

14 Kuhrt, S. (2009), *Church Growth through the Full Welcome of Children: The 'Sssh Free Church'*, Cambridge: Grove Books, p. 9.

15 Hill (2006), *Birthright*, pp. 190, 191.

2

What's in a word?

And the Word became flesh and lived among us, and we have seen his glory, the glory as of a father's only son, full of grace and truth. (John 1.14)

Language forms the bedrock of our human experience, it is the medium in which we live, the means by which we think, the way we make sense of the world and share our experiences with others, 'it is every man's indispensable instrument of thought'.[1] It is the straw with which we build the bricks of our world view, and although each of us can amend and play with language to a small degree, so that it develops and morphs over time, yet we cannot do without it. We find it very difficult even to start to think about something for which we have no language inherited from our social and linguistic group, our forebears and peers.

Language can offer a window into shared values, beliefs and assumptions. By studying how people in a particular group use words, we can gain a greater understanding of what matters to them, what inherited values people work with, either by embracing or reacting against them.

Language and faith

The Bible records how, in many different time periods, cultures and settings, God has engaged with human beings through the medium of language, beginning with creation, in the messages of the prophets, and on to the words of Jesus. By becoming the Word made flesh, God has shown the divine willingness to act within our embodied and language-bound world, to allow Godself to be limited by language in order to communicate with us, a language-bound people.

Of course, our experience of God, as of so many areas of life, also goes beyond words. We do not live in a linguistic cage as some of the more extreme versions of the Sapir-Whorf hypothesis of language and thought suggest. People experience the ineffable divine in 'sighs too deep for words' (Romans 8.26) in prayer, in their visual and aesthetic experiences, in ritual actions and in everyday life: eating, drinking and social interactions. But if the ineffable is to be shared or reflected upon, it needs to be translated into words, into a common language, which limits and shapes our understanding of these experiences. It is perhaps for this reason that it is so easy for human beings to become what Stephen Pattison has called logocentric;[2] to reduce the multifarious religious experiences of human beings to a focus just on doctrines and beliefs, at the expense of actions, relationships and lived experience. This logocentricism appears to be a particular pitfall of religious communities who are inheritors of the Protestant Reformations, as is the case in my own Church, the Church of England. Given this emphasis on words, it is perhaps surprising that the Church has shown such a lack of awareness of its own words, that it has allowed its own language to stray so far from the language with which ordinary people talk about the rite that marks its boundary between insiders and outsiders, the rite of initiation into the Church.

There seems to be a difference of language between churchgoers and the culture at large. However, does this linguistic difference have any theological or sociological significance? Is it just a social quirk, the result of two sections of English society failing to talk to one another enough, or does it represent any more deeply held differences of meaning and theological associations?

Language is more than mere words, if words are to be seen as simply a code to represent a thing in real life. Language is powerful and creative, as seen in the power that the words of God carry in the Bible (Genesis 1; Isaiah 55.1–11). Indeed, in the Johannine view, Jesus himself is seen as the *logos*, the word of God (John 1). John Milbank points out that if God is seen as the *verbum*, and yet language is also understood as a human creation (as seen in Adam naming the animals in Genesis 1), then this could lead to the conclusion that God acts through human culture. As a relational God, God is willing to act in relationship with human beings through the medium of language.[3]

Words in the Bible are seen as creative and powerful but also as potentially destructive (James 3.5–6; Proverbs 18.6–8) and divisive (Genesis 11.1–9). Jesus was the one who brought the inexpressible divine into human society, bringing the message of God in words that the faithful would understand, although also in ones that the theologically educated, 'the wise and the intelligent', would struggle to understand (Matthew 11.25; see also 13.11–16). So, in Jesus, the Word of God, God is seen as becoming present in the ordinary reality of this world. Yet, paradoxically, God still remains inexpressible, beyond the capacity of words to express, a mystery that believers are called to proclaim in worship. Likewise, the Spirit is seen in helping believers in their weakness, interceding on people's behalf when they do not have the words (Romans 8.26).

Christianity is a religion in which words are powerful and influential. Many essential rites have certain words that must be spoken for the ritual action to be seen as valid and effective. Linguists call words that enact the change they describe 'performative utterances'.[4] This is seen in secular life, such as taking on a bet, or naming a ship. But the Christian faith is particularly full of performative utterances, such as the invocation of the Trinity at baptism, the remembrance of the Last Supper at the Eucharist, and the words of blessing from a priest. In the first 1,500 years of the Church's life, these words were accompanied by equally essential ritual actions to produce the sacraments of the Church. While the water of baptism and the bread and wine of the Eucharist remain as essential symbolic elements of the two remaining sacraments in the Protestant churches, the Reformation effected a stripping back of much of the visual and physical elements of the faith which had been essential before, such as the use of images and icons, oil, incense, ritual gestures, crucifixes and rosaries. The Christian traditions that have an inheritance from the Reformation, such as the Church of England, were stripped of the vast majority of their visual, sensory and non-linguistic/non-rational elements. The word became key, ideas became the centre of the faith, Christianity became logocentric.

The decline in religious affiliation in modern times in Western Europe is perhaps best conceived of as a failure of religious language; the traditional inherited ways of talking about God no longer make sense to many people, they do not have the words to describe their spiritual experiences, and so these experiences go undiscussed and unshared.

In Protestant, Western Christian thought we are used to seeing religious experience as essentially an individual affair, a private matter of personal beliefs, or perhaps a personal relationship between a human being and God. But this approach to religion is one that would be alien to the vast majority of people in history and around the world, and it is one that has little appeal to many in modern Britain. Despite the individualism of this age, when people do share spiritual values and seek religious meanings in life, in the overwhelming majority of cases they do so communally, in a way that has been modelled to them and makes sense to them because of their social inheritance. The common language with which these spiritual values, beliefs and attitudes are discussed is, therefore, essential for people to make sense of these ideas. A failure of communication between the Church and society is a failure in mission, preventing the Church from fulfilling its vocation in the world.

Language, baptism and christening

Language featured highly in my thinking about how churchgoers and non-churchgoers had become so separated in their thinking about christenings, and at odds with one another in their understanding of what was going on in the rite. This was partly because of the differences I had observed in how the words themselves (*baptism* or *christening*) were used. But it was also because of more general differences in the ways the families I had visited to prepare them for baptism spoke about the occasion, compared with regular churchgoers. As I began to think about this, I asked people what they thought about these two words. The responses I got supported the impression I had had before I started this research: that regular churchgoers preferred the term *baptism*, whereas non-regular churchgoers preferred *christening*. Some saw the two terms as interchangeable, whereas others had strong feelings of preference for one term or the other. Some had theories about what the difference was between the two. Here's a summary of some of the theories that people proposed for why we have these two different terms for this rite:

- *Baptism* is for adults, whereas *christening* is for children.
- *Baptism* is a more biblical term than *christening*.
- *Christening* relates to the giving of a Christian name.
- *Christening* relates to folk beliefs and traditions.
- *Christening* is seen as old-fashioned by some people, whereas others see *baptism* as old-fashioned.
- *Christening* refers to baptism by aspersion, *baptism* to total immersion.
- Some noted that churchgoers use *baptism*, whereas non-churchgoers use *christening*.
- For a minority of regular churchgoers, especially clergy, there was a strong feeling that *baptism* was the right term and *christening* was the wrong term and indicative of a defective kind of faith, folk religion or superstition.

Many of the clergy I asked about how they saw the difference between the words *baptism* and *christening* argued that *baptism* was a biblical idea, whereas *christening* was a popular construction, full of folk religion (in a derogative sense). However, these assumptions fail to see that neither word is biblical nor unbiblical, since the Bible was not originally written in English. *Christening* is an ancient word, coming from Greek origins just as *baptism* does. It derives from the idea of making a person into a Christian. The next chapter will go into greater depth about the origins and development of the use of these words, but for now we will note how problematic language is with regard to the pastoral and missional practice of baptism in the Church of England today.

The Church of England's Life Events team, led by Sandra Millar, conducted research into the experiences of families who approached a local church to ask for a christening, wedding or funeral. Millar describes beginning the work on baptisms by walking around high streets, looking at christening merchandise and viewing social networking websites, realizing that it is rare, outside church circles, for people to use the word *baptism*.

> An Omnibus survey ... completed as part of the research revealed that for 57 per cent of people the preferred term was ... 'christening', rising to 68 per cent of 35–44-year-olds. It became very clear that to the public this service is called a christening.[5]

The Life Events team found considerable resistance among clergy to its choice to use *christenings* instead of *baptisms* in all their outward-facing material, such as leaflets and their website for families (churchofengland christenings.org). They found they needed to explain this choice carefully to clergy on their inward-facing website, aimed at supporting christening ministry in the churches (churchsupporthub.org).

> One of the most basic decisions has been what to call the project – Baptisms or Christenings? Early indications on social media revealed that there were many, particularly clergy, who objected to the term 'christenings' as dumbing down a theological truth, that the journey begins with baptism and that 'christening' is a subset.[6]

This is put more mildly than by some of the clergy I spoke to, who were deeply disturbed by all that the word *christening* seemed to convey about people's lack of faith and misuse of this rite of the Church. One clergyman, at a conference where I was giving a presentation, for which my title slide contained the word *christening* on a picture of a cake, remarked to me: 'What a disgusting word!' I have encountered this attitude regularly in my ministry. It seems that the word *christening* captures an aspect of modern ministry that Church of England clergy find deeply uncomfortable, arousing feelings of guilt and conflict. I suspect that *christening* is strongly associated in the minds of many English speakers with the less religious, less serious aspects of the rite. *Christening*, it seems, tends to be the word used to describe the cake, the dress, the presents. Meanwhile, *baptism* seems to be used, in church circles, to refer to the actual religious rite, the 'important parts'. I have heard many clergy and active lay people complain that families who want a *christening* are using this sacred rite as an excuse for a party, and have little real understanding of what they are committing themselves to. The work of the Life Events team has done much to help clergy who engage in a more positive way with the language of christenings. It seems many clergy feel that this word is wrong and that it is their duty to oppose it, but Millar's approach has given them permission to use the language of christenings, and in doing so channels of communication have opened up.

> When I stopped worrying about the words they were using, I found I could have real conversations. (Vicar, Rochester diocese)[7]

Beyond the inner circle of committed churchgoers, *christening* often feels a much more natural and comfortable word than *baptism*. The market research commissioned by the Archbishops' Council, which formed the basis of the Life Events team's work, found that 'there was a very strong preference for christening and some confusion over what and whether there was a difference in meaning between the two words'.[8] Some interviewees expressed confusion and concern about which term to use:

> My Mum calls it a Christening, but the Church call it a Baptism, so I'm not really sure which one to use, it depends who I talk to … I had to look it up on the internet, because I wasn't sure. I had read a few different things and I thought, which one is it? [9]

Others created explanations for the language difference, such as this:

> We use christening … Is baptism Catholic and Christening is for Christians?[10]

Whereas some expressed discomfort with using the term *baptism*, for reasons they could not explain:

> Christening. Baptism I don't know, it just doesn't sound right.[11]

One of the interviewees saw *christening* as being a term for younger generations, and *baptism* as being more old-fashioned:

> Christening I think … it seems to be an age thing actually. My father-in-law would say baptism but I've always said christening.[12]

The Omnibus survey referred to by Millar in her book *Life Events* confirmed that this was the case: younger generations are even more likely than average to prefer the word *christening*. This strikes against the impression of some of the regular churchgoers I spoke to, that *christening* was old fashioned.

Overall, the picture I built up prior to carrying out my research was that there is considerable confusion about these two terms, and some (usually well-concealed) negative emotions on the part of many clergy towards those who prefer *christening* to the word they regard as 'right', *baptism*. As an Anglican priest, and even after all this research and improved understanding of the linguistic issues, I still feel somewhat uncomfortable using *christening*. The preference for *baptism* among clergy is very deeply ingrained. The next chapter will show how unsurprising this is as the clerical preference for *baptism* has a history going back as far as the Reformation.

The idea that churchgoers are effectively using a slightly different language from the rest of English culture is not surprising in the light of the work of sociolinguists into differences of language found in sub-cultural groups, including religious groups. These linguistic differences among religious groups can range from the need to have a completely separate, sacred language, such as Arabic or Latin or even speaking in tongues, to understanding a range of particular words or meanings for words in order to fit in with the group, to using a particular cadence or style, as in the traditional Book of Common Prayer or King James Bible-style language used for prayer in some religious communities.

The sociological significance of language

Language can act as a means of defining and distinguishing between different groups within society (linguists call this indexing), making clear the boundaries between groups. This use of language to index groups has been used for millennia, as seen in the use of the pronunciation of 'shibboleth' in the book of Judges (12.5–6) as a means of distinguishing the Gileadites from the Ephraimites by their pronunciation. Many linguists and philosophers have noted the ability of language to divide as well as to unite groups.

> In our culture, in the Pax culturalis to which we are subject, there is an inveterate war of languages: our languages exclude each other; in a society divided (by social class, money, academic origin), language itself divides.[13]

Boundaries and distinctiveness, including linguistic distinctiveness, can be essential in defining and reinforcing a group's sense of identity. It is often possible to tell which religious grouping a person belongs to from linguistic clues, such as the names by which they refer to their church leaders (priest, minister, vicar, reverend). These imply not just a different social allegiance but different models of what Christian leadership means and how it should be deployed.

Groups in society often have 'in-group' and 'out-group' language, which can help to reinforce the identity and sense of worth and distinctiveness for minority groups. Active churchgoers are a good example of this. A 1976 Doctrine Commission report argued that Christian language is bound to be distinctive, and that it 'communicates much more effectively within the community of believers than to those outside'.[14] Not all within the Church of England accept that this is right or inevitable, however. David Cockerell is critical of the idea of Christian community reflected in this report:

> Here the notion of 'community' is contracted and particularized, and religious language is quite explicitly bound up with a dualism between the 'community of believers' and 'those outside', so that its purpose is to articulate the special concerns and interests of the former. Clearly, the more esoteric our conception of religious believing is allowed to become, and thus the more difficult its language to understand, the tighter becomes the distinction between these two groups.[15]

Language matters because, as churchgoers, we have become increasingly unable to communicate effectively with our neighbours. We have used an exclusive language to keep 'outsiders' on the outside, at arm's length, and prevent them from understanding what baptism means to us. Of course, this is the reverse of what most churchgoers actually want, but so often we hope that if we shout loudly enough in church-based language and about the ideas of the Christian faith then those outside will hear and want to come in and learn our language and find out about our faith. But this simply cannot work if the words we use make no sense to those unused to church discourse.

The different 'feels' of baptism and christening in British English

Through constant usage in a variety of ways, words can take on a particular 'feel'. For example, *house* feels very different to *home*, and the verbs *to peddle* or *to sell* are used in very different ways. So, synonyms can be used very differently; they appear frequently in company with other words and in different contexts to one another, and they convey different meanings to native-language speakers. Linguists call this phenomenon of the 'feel' of a word its 'semantic prosody', by which they mean a 'consistent aura of meaning with which a form is imbued',[16] and may refer to 'some kind of evaluative or attitudinal meaning associated with' it.[17]

The British National Corpus is a collection of a huge array of naturally occurring texts, both written and spoken, from the 1990s (see Appendix 2). A search of this corpus for *christening* and *baptism* reveals much about the different 'feels' of these words. Words that occur nearby to a word are called its collocates, and these words can help us to understand the semantic prosody of a word. The top ten collocates (words occurring within four words of it) for *christening* in the British National Corpus are: *baby, dress, silver, party, presents, today, family, godmother, shawl* and *robe/robes*. Meanwhile the top ten collocates for *baptism* are: *fire, infant, Jesus, Christ, marriage, church, burial, confirmation, Spirit* and *holy*. These are strikingly different, and I found similar patterns in other modern British English corpora in my study. *Baptism* tended to appear near to more serious (like *death, funeral* and *burial*) and religious words (like *marriage, confirmation, communion, God, faith* and *Christian*). Meanwhile, *christening* tended to appear nearer to a greater mixture of words with practical and social resonance, and often a celebratory tone (like *baby, party, gift, wedding, drunk*). The strong association of *baptism* with *fire*, of course, comes from the common use of the figure of speech 'baptism of fire'. This, in itself, shows how *baptism* has a more challenging 'feel' to British English speakers than *christening* does, speaking of suffering and trials. Interestingly, godparents are more strongly associated, linguistically, with *christening* than with *baptism*. The significance of this will be explored in Chapter 6.

Given the seriousness, even danger, associated with the word *baptism*, along with the tendency for it to be used more by those of higher social standing and especially by clergy (which will be argued in the next chapter), it is perhaps far from surprising that those who do not go to church regularly may feel uncomfortable about using it. The Church has been promoting *baptism* as the correct way to refer to this rite since before the Reformation, but in doing this we have been pushing parishioners towards a word that feels deeply challenging, negative even, associated with death, fire and suffering, and away from a word that feels positive, *christening*, associated with family and celebration.

In many ways this is far from inappropriate. After all, Jesus used *baptism* as a euphemism for suffering and death (Mark 10.38), and Paul argued that baptism is, in part, an immersion into and ritual identification with the death of Christ (Romans 6.3). Baptism should not be easy, becoming a Christian is costly and a serious commitment (Luke 14.25–33). But the danger with the Church's insistence on using *baptism* and rejecting *christening* as a way of referring to this rite is that, from the very start when people are just dipping their toes in the water of faith, we put them off unintentionally by not understanding the impact of our language, because we in the Church use language in a different way to those who are not part of our church communities. Whether or not we choose to offer a christening to those who come to ask, we need to be aware of what it is that they are seeking, what it means to them, and to know the real value of this.

Using language as a window to understand people's religious worlds

We have seen that language is deeply significant, both theologically and socially. I have used a study of language about this rite as a way of understanding what it means to people, both within and beyond the Church in England. This is an unusual methodology for practical theology (see Appendix 1 for more details on the methods used in this research), but one that I have found very fruitful, giving unique insights into the place of christenings within English society. The next chapter will explore how the language and understanding of baptism has changed over time and what this may tell us about how people understand and relate to this essential sacrament of the Church, both in the past and today.

Notes

1 Piaget, J. (1968), *Structuralism*, trans. and ed. by Chaninah Maschler, London: Routledge & Kegan Paul, p. 75.

2 Pattison, S. (2007), *Seeing Things: Deepening Relations with Visual Artefacts*, London: SCM Press, p. 15.

3 Milbank, J. (1997), *The Word Made Strange: Theology, Language, Culture*, Oxford: Blackwell, p. 80.

4 Austin, J. L. (1976), *How to Do Things with Words*, 2nd edn, Oxford: Clarendon Press, p. 6.

5 Millar, S. (2018), *Life Events: Mission and Ministry at Baptisms, Weddings and Funerals*, London: Church House Publishing, p. 30.

6 Millar, S. (2014), 'Christening or Baptism?', Church Support Hub website,

Church of England. Retrieved 13.6.2017, from https://churchsupporthub.org/article/christening-baptism/.

7 Millar (2018), *Life Events*, p. 31.

8 9Dot Research (2013), *Christening Matters Research Report*, Kettering: Church of England, p. 7.

9 9Dot Research (2013), *Christening Matters*, p. 7.

10 9Dot Research (2013), *Christening Matters*, p. 7.

11 9Dot Research (2013), *Christening Matters*, p. 7.

12 9Dot Research (2013), *Christening Matters*, p. 7.

13 Barthes, R. and Howard, R. (1986), *The Rustle of Language*, Oxford: Basil Blackwell, p. 101.

14 The Doctrine Commission of the Church of England (1976), *Christian Believing: The Nature of the Christian Faith and its Expression in Holy Scripture and Creeds*, London: SPCK, p. 15.

15 Cockerell, D. (1989), *Beginning Where We Are: A Theology of Parish Ministry*, London: SCM Press, p. 8.

16 Louw, B. (1993), 'Irony in the Text or Insincerity in the Writer? The Diagnostic Potential of Semantic Prosodies', in M. Baker, G. Francis, E. Tognini-Bonelli and J. M. Sinclair (eds), *Text and Technology: In Honour of John Sinclair*, Philadelphia: J. Benjamins Pub. Co., p. 157.

17 Mahlberg, M. (2014), 'Corpus Stylistics', in M. Burke (ed.), *The Routledge Handbook of Stylistics*, London: Routledge, p. 383.

3

The history of 'baptism' and 'christening' in the English language

How has the use of the words *baptism* (along with related words like *baptized* and *baptismal*) and *christening* (*christen, christened* and so on), changed over time? For a start, *christen* is older in the English language than *baptism*. To *christen* is an old Anglo-Saxon word going back to the pre-Norman conquest era, whereas *baptism* came into the language around the fourteenth century. From early on in its history, *baptism* has been a word with loftier associations than *christening*, being used to talk about the theology of the sacrament, whereas *christening* was used in Reformation-era England to refer to the practical side of initiation. These differences in origins have had, and continue to have, an impact upon the ways the words are used and what they mean. Their use has varied according to social class and level of formality of speech or writing, with those of lower social class using *christening* more and those of higher social class, and in more formal circumstances, using *baptism* more, as far back as the seventeenth century. In the twenty-first century there is still a marked social difference in the choice of words to talk about the rite. Between 1995 and 2015, red-top tabloid newspapers were much more likely to refer to a *christening*, whereas broadsheet newspapers more often chose to call the rite a *baptism*. By the twentieth and twenty-first century, language about this rite in church circles was almost entirely dominated by the word *baptism* and devoid of the word *christening*. This preference is very deep rooted, being the normal language of clergy as far back as the sixteenth century. The animosity of clergy towards the word *christening* reflects an entrenched suspicion of the religious practices of ordinary people, which has persisted for at least 400 years, perhaps longer.

Old English (*c.* 450–1100)

Old English was the language of the Anglo-Saxons, derived from the Germanic roots of the migratory people, the Angles, Saxons and Jutes.

It has been given various date ranges, and, naturally, the evolution from Old English into Middle English was gradual, sparked by the Norman invasion of 1066.

Old English had a variety of words to refer to specific aspects of the rites of Christian initiation. One set of words were based on the word *cristen*, meaning 'Christian' as well as the rite that makes a person into a Christian (baptism), for example, *cristennes* (meaning baptism, Christian or Christianity). Another set were based on the word stem *ful*, such as *fullwiht* (meaning baptism) and *fantwæter* (meaning the water used at baptism). These *ful-* words were classic Anglo-Saxon compound words, where *ful* means 'brimming over' and *wiht* means 'at all' or 'completely'.[1]

Cristen is an example of a small group of loanwords in Old English, which means that they were borrowed from another language. Loanwords were much less common in Old English than in modern English, with one estimate being that only 3 per cent of Old English words were borrowed from other languages, whereas 70 per cent of modern English words are loanwords.[2] *Cristen* was among a group of about 450 loanwords brought into Old English from Latin by the first Christian missionaries. Most of these words have religious uses (*altar, cleric, nun, temple,* etc.). Old English did not have our modern word *baptism*.

Middle English (*c.* 1100–1500)

The Norman aristocracy introduced a large number of loanwords into the English language from Old French, spoken by the Normans, which caused a period of rapid change in the English language. Among the new words were the words *baptize* and *bapteme*, which were used alongside variants on the older words *cristen* and *fulwiht*, to refer to the rite of initiation. Perhaps because this new word referred only to the rite itself, and not also to being a Christian, as well as because of its higher social standing as a French-derived word, it came to be the word favoured for theoretical discussions of baptism and for Bible translations.

Although both *christening* and *baptism* are loanwords, the different ways they came to be absorbed into the English language has had an enduring impact upon their prestige and use. The form of the words reveals their origins: *Christen* ends with the morpheme *-en*, meaning 'to become', which comes from Old English. Meanwhile, *baptize* ends with the morpheme *-ize*, meaning 'to cause to be X', which comes from French.[3] Loanwords that were imported into the English language from the French in the Middle English period often carried, and still carry, a higher social status, as they came from the language of the ruling elite.

As many of the records surviving from this period were penned by monks and priests, often from the ruling elite Norman French-speaking families, it is hard to tell how quickly the much more numerous Anglo-Saxon population took up these new words. Minkova and Stockwell argue that the fact that most of the writing was undertaken by the Norman elite 'might conceal both potential negative attitudes and the rate at which new words were actually adopted by speakers of English. Thus, an early record of a French word is no guarantee that that word was familiar and current throughout the linguistic community.'[4]

The changes in these terms were reflective of changes occurring throughout the English language at this time. The new borrowed words in Middle English were instrumental in transforming the English language from a language of the common folk, while all matters of state and religion were conducted in Latin, to a language which was considered (by some people by the end of this period) as being complex and sophisticated enough to be appropriate for use in worship, Bible reading and government. This change was controversial at the time of the Reformation (just after the end of the Middle English period) and very few considered using English in these ways in the Middle English period, other than a few revolutionary thinkers such as Wycliffe.

The introduction of French loanwords allowed new concepts to be given words to describe them and also increased 'synonymy in the language, thus providing alternative ways of saying the same thing in different registers'.[5] This introduction of different lexical levels within the language, some words carrying higher or lower social status, can also be seen as having introduced a kind of 'lexical bar',[6] by which those from humble backgrounds are often kept from moving up socially because they are not familiar with the higher prestige loanwords, a division that persists in the social world of today's British English speakers.

In 1382, Wycliffe published his controversial translation of the Bible into English. In just the third chapter of the New Testament, in Matthew 3, Wycliffe chose the word that would have been most familiar to native English speakers, *christened*, to talk about the rituals of John the Baptist in the Jordan, in combination with the new word *baptism*. This word would have been unfamiliar to most native English speakers at the time; the *Oxford English Dictionary* only has one earlier use (just five years earlier, in Langland's *Piers Plowman* of 1377). Wycliffe seems to have introduced the new word by combining it with the more familiar word, *christened*.

Then Jerusalem went out to him, and all Jude, and all the country about Jordan; And they were **christened** (**cristenyd**) of him in Jordan, acknowledging their sins. Soothly he seeing many of Pharisees and of Sadducees coming to his **baptism** (**bapteme**), said to him, Generations of eddris, who showed to you for to flee from wrath to come? ... Then Jesus came from Galilee in to Jordan to John, for to be **christened** (**cristned**) of him. Soothly John forbid him, saying I owe to be **christened** (**cristned**) of thee, and thou commest to me? (Matthew 3.5–7, 13, 14, from Wycliffe's translation of the Bible)[7]

In this version, in Matthew 3, Wycliffe uses *christened* more often than *baptized*. However, in the later Gospels' accounts of the baptism of Jesus, he mainly uses *baptized*, although *christened* was given as an alternative in John 3.22, and is used in Acts 18.8 and Luke 3.21. This might be because he translated the New Testament over an extended period, during which the word *baptism* was in the process of being introduced into the English language. Alternatively, it could reflect a conscious effort on Wycliffe's part to introduce the unfamiliar technical word for the rite to the English-speaking population.

Wycliffe's friend and colleague John Purvey published a revised edition of the Bible after Wycliffe's death, around 1395. In this new version, almost all of the occurrences of the word *christened* were replaced either with the verbs *baptized* or *washed*. Just one occurrence of *christened* was retained, in Acts 18.8. This instance of *christened* was perhaps allowed to remain because the baptism referred to here was specifically about conversion of the Corinthians to Christianity. Conversion, especially of adults, was at this stage particularly strongly linked to the word *christened*, since it helpfully conveyed both the meaning of undergoing the rite of initiation and also being made a Christian (which at this stage was the same word, *a christen*). These changes, in just 13 years, reflect a fast-changing language at this stage of its evolution. *Baptism* had, early in the Middle English period, come to be the only proper word to use to refer to this rite in the Bible. However, this was not inevitable, and the development of Wycliffe's Bible suggests that the use of *baptism* needed to be introduced gradually to an English-speaking population that still regarded the new word as novel.

Early Modern English (1500–1700)

The period traditionally designated as Early Modern English began at a time of great turmoil and upheaval for the English nation and the English language. The invention of the printing press made texts much more widely available, and monasteries lost their monopoly on the dissemination of books. English-language texts were gradually becoming more common, as Latin receded as the language of state. Early on in this period the Reformation brought a massive importation of ideas, and also words, from the Continent.

From 1500 to the present day, of all the wide range of texts that I looked at in detail, I found very few serious uses of the word *christening* by clergy. However, in the sixteenth century this low rate of use of the word *christening* among clergy may have been due more to the type of texts than indicative that they did not use the term in everyday speech. After all, the official baptismal records of the Church at this stage were called registers of *christenings*, so they could hardly have completely avoided its use. The reason that the clergy rarely used *christening* in these texts is perhaps mainly because they rarely referred in writing to the practice of baptism, which was the circumstance in which, in the sixteenth and seventeenth centuries, it was appropriate to use *christening*. They were much more likely to discuss baptism in a more abstract way, such as in biblical quotations or allusions, sacramental or theological discussions, for which at this period it was most appropriate to choose to use the word *baptism*.

> Whosoever are **christened** (**chrystened**) they have put on Christ first ... children therefore before they receive Christ they must be **christened** .... **baptism** (**baptyme**) for us in the new law is counted in the stead of circumcision ... Children therefore must of necessity be **christened** that **baptism** (**baptysme**) to us in the law is in the stead of circumcision. (Lancelot Ridley, 1540)[8]

This pattern of usage of these words is shown well in this quotation, where Lancelot Ridley, a clergyman of evangelical persuasions in the early years of the English Reformation, uses *christened* liberally to talk about the rite, but switches to *baptism* when talking about it in a theoretical sense. It is interesting here that the word *christened* is always a verb and *baptism* is a noun, reflecting the fact that the former was used in active situations (to talk about the practice of christening), and the latter when talking about baptism as a thing in the abstract. This distinction does not hold out in all language of this time period, but it is not uncommon to see this pattern in the sixteenth century and in Middle English, as in the quotation from Matthew 3 in Wycliffe's Bible above.

Figure 1 is created from the massive database of Middle English and Early Modern English texts known as EEBO (Early English Books Online; see Appendix 2 for more details). An n-gram like this is created from an electronic search of this database for particular words, in this case all

Figure 1: EEBO n-gram for baptized *and* christened *(as verbs)*[9]

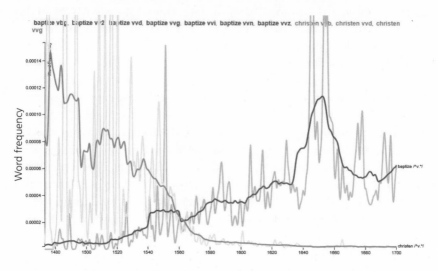

spelling variants of *baptized* and *christened* as verbs, the darker grey line showing *baptized* and the lighter grey line showing *christened*. It shows that *christened* was more commonly used in these texts to talk about this rite up until about 1550 (just 16 years since the Act of Supremacy), after which *baptized* took over as the most common verb to describe the rite.

The timing of this, just after the Reformation, is no coincidence. The influx of new ideas from the Continent seems to have fuelled rapid language change. This is demonstrated by Figure 2, which compares the use of these words among Protestant and Catholic writers in the period 1500–70.[10]

Catholic writers had much the same pattern of linguistic use as had been the norm up to this point in the English language, which is to use *baptism* and *christening* in fairly equal amounts, but most often to use *christen* to mean 'a Christian'. Protestant writers, on the other hand, appear to have been early adopters of the new word *Christian*, using *christen* to mean 'Christian' much less than other English speakers in the same period. In addition, they used *baptism* much more often than the traditional word *christening*, compared with others in this period. Again, this shows Protestant writers in the vanguard of linguistic change, as later periods saw the rise of the use of the word *baptism*, and the gradual decline in the use of *christening*, at least among the intellectual elite of the population. The use of *christen* to mean 'a Christian' disappeared almost entirely by the end of the sixteenth century.

Figure 2: Word usage in texts, 1500–70, by religious group

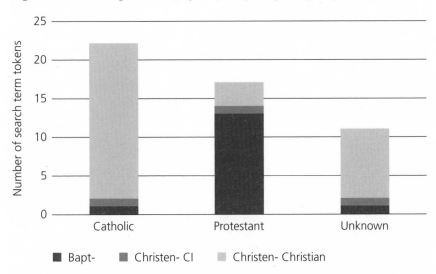

After the Reformation, the distinction between the two words used to refer to this rite gradually broke down, as *baptized* began to be used to refer to the action of baptizing a person, as well as to the concept of baptism. In the seventeenth century, the distinction weakened, and it finally broke down altogether in the eighteenth century. The reason for the expanded meaning of *baptism* at this time appears to have been due to the reticence of some people, especially clergymen and keen Protestants, to use the word *christening*, leading to the very gradual erosion of the credibility of the word.

An active dislike of the word *christening* was rare in the sixteenth century, but it was seen occasionally in some texts by the end of the century, as in the quotation below, where Gentillet implies that the word is the preserve of Catholics, even though he himself uses it elsewhere in this text. He does this in the context of a Catholic practice he regards as repugnant, namely to allow women to baptize *in extremis*.

> Again, whereas the Catholics enable women to **baptise** (which they call **christening**) in doing whereof they commit unto them one of the chief charges in gods house. (Gentillet, 1579)[11]

Why did the word *christening*, albeit only in some writings and for some people, become associated with Catholicism in the late sixteenth and seventeenth centuries? It was not a universal association, nor was *christening* abandoned altogether and fully replaced by *baptism*. But the association between *christening* and Catholicism was occasionally made by those who wished to attack Catholic religion by associating it with the earthier, more practical aspects of the rite. Throughout the sixteenth century, *christening* was almost universally associated with practice, *baptism* with the theoretical aspects of initiation. *Baptism* therefore reflected all that was considered loftiest and most exalted about the rite: the Bible, sacraments and theology. These aspects were the preserve of university-educated men talking about the theory of God and his relationship with the Church. *Christening*, meanwhile, was used more by women and was used to talk about practical matters, the aspects of the rite that could easily be looked down upon by some. Lay people, including the uneducated and those of humble origins, were able to have a degree of control over their christenings. Godparents, ordinary lay people, were considered to be instrumental in christening a child (see Chapter 6). *Christening* spoke of all the aspects of the rite over which lay people, however low their social status, were able to have an influence. *Baptism*, on the other hand, spoke of all the elements over which clergy had control. So, in portraying *christening* as the word used by Catholics, Gentillet was implying that Catholic faith is lowly, untheological and uneducated, perhaps even superstitious, earthly and unspiritual.

> The Long Reformation involved an effort by religious and political leaders to centralize authority. Reformers attempted to wrest authority from laypeople by greatly reducing the local and particularistic religious practices that had allowed nonauthorized laypersons immediate access to the sacred. The contested boundaries between sacred and profane were often at the core of this effort.[12]

Before the Reformation, the Church jealously defended its authority over theology and the ability to interpret Scripture; access to it was limited through restricting the Bible and theological discussions of it to the scholarly language of Latin. It was only clergymen who performed the sacraments (baptism being an exception to this in extreme circumstances). Theologically, the rite of initiation belonged to the Church, and its interpretation of the nature of the rite was conducted using the word *baptism*. However, in terms of practice, in terms of local traditions, folk practices, the use of symbolism, social celebrations and the formation of spiritual kin networks, the Church allowed people much more freedom than was the case after the Reformation. It was these aspects of the rite that were most strongly associated with *christening*, and it appears to have been these aspects that many Protestants, and most clergymen, were trying to move away from by avoiding using *christening* and instead extending the meaning of *baptism* to cover the practice of the rite of initiation, not just the theory of it.

A closer look at Figure 1 reveals that times of religious and political turmoil coincided with peaks of interest in the rite of Christian initiation. This and other EEBO n-gram analyses of the use of these words as nouns[13] reveal a peak in the use of both *baptism* and *christening* during the 1550s and 1560s. This peak coincided with the fraught times during reigns of the three children of Henry VIII, when the country lurched from extreme Protestant reforms to Catholic restoration and back to Protestantism within just over a decade, so it is unsurprising that baptism and Christian identity was an important theme at this stage. Another peak of interest in this rite is seen in a later period of high religious tension, around 1650, after the execution of Charles I in 1649, when the country was ruled by the strongly Puritan parliament during the Commonwealth period. However, while use of *baptism* peaked around 1650 in the EEBO texts, this peak coincided with a dip in the use of the word *christening*. This shows the fast decrease in the status of the word *christening* between the sixteenth and seventeenth centuries. In the former, *christening* was a valid term to refer to this rite and its use peaked along with its counterpart, *baptism*, in response to increased religious tensions. But, by the seventeenth century, *christening* had become almost an anti-religious word in the minds of some of the religious elite in society, and, in times of religious tension, this time *baptism* was used more and *christening* less.

The stage was set for *baptism* to take over *christening* as the main way that clergy talked about this rite. In the following centuries, this preference for *baptism* over *christening* would spread from the clergy to other people of higher social status, professional people and the upper classes. But, at this stage, most people still used the older word *christening* much more frequently, and people of lower social status continued to do so throughout the eighteenth and nineteenth centuries.

Eighteenth and nineteenth centuries

The eighteenth century could be seen as the calm after the storm of the Civil War, Commonwealth, Restoration and Glorious Revolution. As religious control of the population loosened, dissent blossomed and became a strong feature of the religious landscape of England. It was the time before the French Revolution shook Europe's political and religious worlds.

A rich seam of evidence for language use in this period is found in the records of the trials that took place in the Old Bailey, in a periodical that records the words used at the proceedings of the criminal trials. Along with the texts from this periodical, the Old Bailey Proceedings website also includes another periodical, the *Ordinary's Accounts*, which was published by the chaplains of Newgate prison from 1676 to 1772. The *Ordinary's Accounts* detailed the chaplains' accounts of their conversations with those condemned to hang at Tyburn. An analysis of the words used by these clergymen shows that they were vastly different from the patterns of words found among ordinary people in the records of the trials at the Old Bailey. In the trials, in the eighteenth century, all types of people used *christening* much more often than *baptism*. The patterns of language among the chaplains of Newgate, however, were very different. The *Ordinary's Accounts* contain long quotations from the chaplains, retelling the words of the condemned in their conversations with them, but in the two 20-year periods that I studied in detail, the prisoners (and others quoted by the chaplains) were reported as using *baptism* 19 times, but *christening* only twice.[14] It seems the chaplains of Newgate 'corrected' the prisoners' words to reflect their own language, that is, to use *baptized* instead of *christened*. On the two occasions that *christening* appears in the time periods studied from the *Ordinary's Accounts*, once it is in a letter from a prisoner (and so is in his own words), and the other time it refers to a practice that the chaplain clearly regarded as not true baptism, since he afterwards baptized the prisoner:

> William Ogilvie, two days before he died, told me, that he often heard his mother say, she believed he never was **baptized**, and that, if I thought convenient, he would be very glad to have that ceremony performed on him by me. In consequence of which I conformed with his desire, having first sent for his mother, who informed me, that his father, a freethinker, and very great libertine, took him, when an infant, from her lying in bed, and said he would have him **christened** after his own manner, for he would not have any thing to do with those people who were called ministers; and as she was uncertain whether he ever was **baptized**, begged that I would comply with her son's request. (John Wood, 1770)[15]

In the *Ordinary's Accounts*, the chaplains' retelling of the words they used when speaking to prisoners showed much less variation than their account of the words used by the prisoners, with the overwhelming focus being on the theoretical discussion of baptism, whereas the prisoners' words reveal much more interest in the practice of the rite and the importance of it as a definer of identity. This difference shows how the language of the eighteenth century is carrying on the patterns seen in the sixteenth and seventeenth centuries, in which clerical language focused on the theoretical aspects of the rite. Again, the practical and popular aspects of the rite are less elevated, while the theoretical are emphasized and form a much greater focus of interest for clergymen in this period.

By comparing the words of witnesses, victims and defendants (WVD) on the one hand with the group of lawyers, professional witnesses and the words of the clerk who recorded the trial proceedings (LPT) on the other, the records of the trials at the Old Bailey can show differences in language use according to social level. This is because the WVD group mainly consisted of lower-ranking people, who got involved in crime, whereas the LPT group were all professional or high-ranking men and women. The WVD group has the unusual advantage of having almost as many women as men. It is rare to have such a rich source of female spoken language from the eighteenth and nineteenth centuries. Unfortunately, the same is not true of the LPT group, which is overwhelmingly (but not exclusively) male. The language of both groups is in a formal, spoken register, consistent with speech in the formal setting of a law court.

In the eighteenth century, those with higher social prestige (the LPT group of professional men, shown as a dotted line in Figure 3) used

Figure 3: Old Bailey Proceedings, use of baptism *as opposed to* christening *for each group over time*

baptism slightly more than the lower social group (WVDs, shown as a dashed line for men and a solid line for women), and within this group men used *baptism* more than women. However, all used *christening* more than *baptism*, and the differences between the groups was fairly small. So, *baptism* was used more by those of higher social status (men compared with women, and professional men compared with other men), but, for all, *christening* was the main word used. This is not surprising, due to the predominantly practical nature of these texts, as *christening* had been the preferred term to talk about the practice of initiation in previous centuries, as we have already seen.

Certificates and registers were more usually referred to as registers of *christenings* rather than of *baptism* in the eighteenth century, which was a continuation of the practice in Early Modern English. However, the eighteenth century was a time of great linguistic change, and by the end of the century, and into the nineteenth century, great changes were observed in the pattern of language in the Old Bailey Proceedings.

> In terms of the development of the national language, the late eighteenth century saw a marked acceleration of the process of codification. The elaboration of a prescriptive grammar, an obsession with logical rule, and a clearer separation out of the 'vulgar' and 'polite' tongues were all characteristic.[16]

By the middle of the three periods sampled (1781–1850), the use of *christening* suddenly declined in social acceptance among the elite. This was reflected in the sudden change of official records, which were now referred to as registers and certificates of *baptism*, and in the abrupt change in the choice of words among the higher-ranking LPT group, who changed from mainly using *christening* in the eighteenth century to mainly using *baptism* by the late eighteenth and early nineteenth century. Meanwhile the lower-ranking WVD group only very slightly increased their use of *baptism*, resulting in a widening gap between the way that lower- and higher-ranking people talked about this sacrament, which is clearly shown in Figure 3. Interestingly, women's increase in the use of *baptism* was greater than men in this period, perhaps reflecting the tendency of women to be drivers of linguistic change.[17]

New figurative uses of both words were seen in the late eighteenth century, especially in the *christening* of watches or clocks, which means changing the name on them to hide the fact that they are stolen and/or increase their value (a use noted in the 'dictionary of the vulgar tongue' in 1811).[18] *Baptism* was also used in figurative ways not seen before, such as in the naming of people or objects. This tendency to develop new figurative uses of these words was also seen in the records of debates in the Houses of Parliament (Hansard; see Appendix 2) in the nineteenth century. However, some of the now familiar figurative uses of these words, such as *baptism of fire*, were not known until later on in the nineteenth century and only became common at the very end of this century and into the twentieth century.

The changing use and status of these words appears to have led to confusion among people of lower social status, as seen in the four mentions among WVDs in the Old Bailey Proceedings of *half-baptism*, a practice that appears to refer to an act of baptism in the home when a child is in danger of death.[19] This was seen as being completed by *full christening* in church at a later point. In the minds of the mostly low-social-ranking WVDs, this shows that *christening* is still the 'proper' word for this rite, but the clergy's insistence on using *baptism* to describe the ceremony they perform *in extremis* has perhaps resulted in this theologically questionable idea of half and full baptism, as seen in the following quotation from a witness asked about the age of a child when they were baptized: 'About a twelve month old when he was full **christened**; he was half **baptized** first' (Esther Kirby, 1793, witness at trial of Joseph Southflat).[20]

The gulf between the language of lower-ranking (WVD) people and higher-ranking (LPT) men that had opened up in the late eighteenth and early nineteenth century widened still further in the latter half of the nineteenth century (as seen in Figure 3 above). The lower-ranking group did increase their use of *baptism*, and decrease the proportion of times they chose to use *christening*, but the latter was still by far the preferred term, contrary to the practice of the higher-ranking group in this period. Meanwhile, on the few occasions that clergy appeared as witnesses in these trials, they continued the pattern seen in the texts analysed in the Early Modern English period, and in the *Ordinary's Accounts*, of almost entirely avoiding use of the word *christening*.

Clergy language in the sixteenth and seventeenth centuries could be seen as an extreme version of university-educated, male and Protestant language. By the nineteenth century, clerical language had become an extreme version of the language of higher-status individuals and professional men. The great divide between *baptism* and *christening* was now well established, allowing very different associations and feelings to become associated with these words. Official records by the nineteenth century were almost universally known as *baptism registers*, whereas parties and objects such as gifts and robes were described using the word *christening*.

In the nineteenth century, the practical, administrative role that christenings had always fulfilled, in registering a child's parentage, date and place of birth and names, was removed by the 1836 Births and Deaths Registrations Act. Thus, while it took some time for all people to see it this way (as explored in more detail in Chapter 4), it became possible for a child to have a name, to officially recognize their parents and to prove their existence in society without baptism. The elements of the rite that were associated with the word *christening*, the practical matters pertaining to the birth of a child and their reception into society, were being stripped away from the elements that the Church wished to emphasize and give dignity to, the religious elements more closely associated with the word *baptism*. Prior to the nineteenth century, the administrative, practical, social and spiritual elements of a christening had been inseparable. When the Act was proposed, many people in the Houses of Parliament found it difficult to see how it was possible for these things to be separated from baptism. Yet, despite the fact that the Church bemoaned the removal of these functions, the separation had already been initiated by the Church's push to embrace *baptism* and to reject *christening* in the seventeenth and eighteenth centuries. Clergymen had downplayed and mocked *christening*, associating it with the practical, social and emotional aspects of the rite. Instead, clergymen had favoured *baptism*, which related only to the spiritual and intellectual aspects. Baptism itself was being gradually changed, stripped of its practical and social roles, very slowly becoming one sided and less rooted in the English culture and in people's lives, such that roles that it was once uniquely able to fulfil in the life of society could be conceived of becoming separated and secularized, as they were as a result of the 1836 Registrations Act.

Twentieth- and twenty-first centuries

The twentieth century saw a continuation of many of the trends seen in earlier centuries. The use of *christening* continued to decline through most of the twentieth century, and *baptism* continued to be the preferred term among higher social groups, and most obviously in church circles. This church-based preference for *baptism* over *christening* was by far the most marked trend and persisted until the end of the study (around 2016). Similarly, well into the twenty-first century there was still a social differential in the use of these words to talk about the rite of initiation, with higher social groups using *baptism* more and lower social groups using *christening* more. But there were also new trends, especially the considerable rise in figures of speech using these terms as the twentieth century progressed. One of the most often used meanings for *christening* was as a figure of speech to refer to naming (e.g. 'they christened the dog

Ben'). And one of the most frequently used meanings of *baptism* was in the figure of speech *baptism of fire*, and variants on this theme. Another change was the overall increase in the use of *christening* from the 1990s onwards, even in more formal language such as in speeches in the Houses of Parliament. While the social patterns already noted remained into the twenty-first century, all groups, including in more formal language and among higher social groups, began to use *christening* more than they did earlier in the twentieth century and in earlier centuries. This is seen especially in the Hansard records of speeches made in the Houses of Parliament, as Figure 4 shows.

The Hansard records belong to a very specialized genre, giving evidence of the highly stylized and formal speech of elite people. This corpus is particularly useful in that it allows a comparison of language of a single genre over a long period of time (1803–2005). A comparison of words used to refer directly to the rite of initiation (rather than as a figure of speech or to refer to naming) confirms what would be expected from

Figure 4: Baptism *and* christening *used to mean Christian initiation in Hansard, records of debates in the Houses of Parliament*

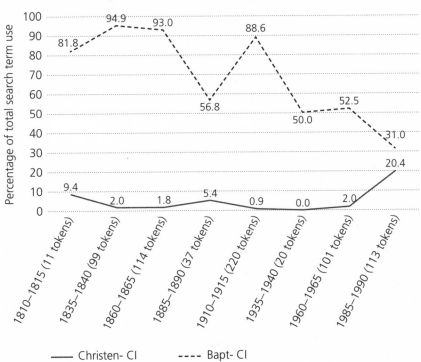

31

earlier centuries, that these high-status people in this highly formal setting used *baptism*, rather than *christening*, almost all the time to refer
to this rite. This trend continued into the early twentieth century, when
two changes occurred. First, these words were used more often in other
ways, such as to refer to naming, or as figures of speech, and the subject
of Christian initiation became less of a common topic in the Houses of
Parliament. The 1910s saw a final peak of interest in baptism due to the
introduction of the old-age pension, requiring people to prove their age
to claim this. As many of those in old age in the 1910s had been born
prior to the 1836 Registration Act, certificates of baptism were referred
to regularly in the debates over the pension at this stage. Meanwhile,
towards the end of the nineteenth century, it became increasingly fashion-
able to use *christened* to mean figuratively named, rising to a quarter of
all uses of these words in 1960–65 and 20 per cent in 1985–90. In addition, *baptism* was used in more figurative senses from the late nineteenth
century, rising to over a quarter of all search-term use from 1985 to
1990. These figurative uses became increasingly elaborate and clever, as
seen in the quotations below:

> nobody would have called him anything except Lord Hartington. No-
> body would have called him Mr. Cavendish. However, I do not think
> that this is of any great importance. I am bound to say that, logical as it
> may be, it does not seem to me that there is any significant grace which
> attaches to this rather odd form of **baptismal** regeneration. (The Earl of
> Swinton, 1963, House of Lords)[21]

> It must give the noble Lord some special satisfaction to act as god-
> parent at this Bill's **baptism**, so I hope that no one will be pouring too
> much cold water on it. (Lord Hesketh, 1989, House of Lords)[22]

The other change that took place, from the 1960s onwards, was the
resurgence in the use of the word *christening* to refer to the rite of initiation in this highly formal language of social elites. *Baptism* was still by
far the most commonly used word, but the gap was closing, and by the
1980s *christening* was being used almost as often as *baptism* to refer to
the rite in Hansard.

However, the Hansard corpus provides evidence of only one, very specialized, genre of speech. The British National Corpus provides evidence
of texts, including speech, from many different genres in the 1990s. This
massive collection of text samples from a huge range of sources, collected
for language analysis purposes in the 1900s, is helpful as 10 per cent of
the texts come from speech, including transcripts of conversations, radio

programmes, meetings, sermons, etc. I was able to separate out analysis of this part of the corpus into speech in a church context (such as transcripts of church meetings or sermons) from that in secular contexts (such as conversations or radio programmes). Figures 5 and 6 show every occurrence of the search terms (*christen, christened, christening, baptism,*

Figure 5: Baptism *and* christening *in spoken church contexts in the British National Corpus (% of total of 105 tokens)*

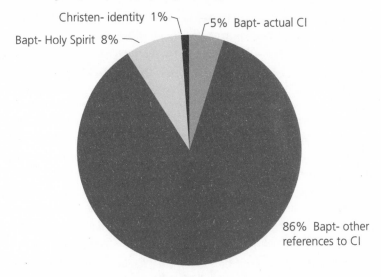

Christen- identity 1%
Bapt- Holy Spirit 8%
5% Bapt- actual CI
86% Bapt- other references to CI

Figure 6: Baptism *and* christening *in spoken secular contexts in the British National Corpus (% of total of 61 tokens)*

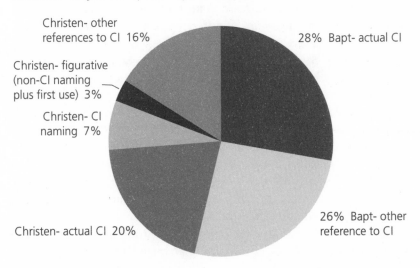

Christen- other references to CI 16%
Christen- figurative (non-CI naming plus first use) 3%
Christen- CI naming 7%
Christen- actual CI 20%
28% Bapt- actual CI
26% Bapt- other reference to CI

baptize, baptismal, etc.) in the spoken element of the British National Corpus, categorized by word type (*bapt-* or *christen-*) and by use (to refer to Christian initiation (CI), naming, as an indicator of identity, as a figure of speech, etc.). A comparison of Figure 5 (church context speech) with Figure 6 (secular contexts speech) reveals that these words are used in very different ways in church-based speech compared to speech in everyday life. The starkest difference is in the balance of use of *baptism* compared to *christening*, with the latter being used only once in a church context in the entire spoken element of the corpus, but in the non-church contexts *christening* is used almost as often as *baptism*. Also, in the non-church contexts, both words are used much more often to refer to the rite itself, showing that the interest in theoretical discussion of baptism seen by clergy in earlier periods continues into modern times in church-based speech. Similarly, the mainly practical and pragmatic interest in the rite among laity seen in earlier periods also continues into everyday speech in contemporary secular contexts. Also interesting is the complete lack of figurative uses of these words, or uses of them to refer to naming, in the church-based speech in Figure 5, while these uses are seen in non-church-based speech in Figure 6.

This difference between church-based language and secular language is perhaps most clearly demonstrated in the study of newspapers from 1995 to 2015 (see Appendix 2 for full details of newspapers and time periods studied). In the two church newspapers studied (*Church Times* and *Church of England Newspaper*), *christening* was used just 8 per cent of the time and *baptism* 92 per cent.[23] By contrast, among the secular newspapers, the use of these words was roughly equal. This was true for broadsheet newspapers as well as for tabloids and red-top tabloids newspapers. However, this hides an important social difference between newspapers aimed at readerships of different social levels, since the newspapers tended to use these words in different ways. Red-top tabloids were particularly likely to use *baptism* figuratively, especially in the phrase *baptism of fire*, which comprised 38 per cent of these words used in the *Sun* newspaper. *Christening*, meanwhile, was frequently used in the broadsheet newspapers to refer to naming. In *The Guardian* 26 per cent of word use was to refer to the figurative naming of objects and people (not at baptism). When these other uses are stripped out, and use to refer to the rite of initiation is compared, a stark social difference appears.

Figure 7 illustrates how the social split seen in the Old Bailey trial records, emerging in the eighteenth century and opening up into a huge gulf in the nineteenth and early twentieth centuries, was still very much apparent in the early twenty-first century. When talking about the rite itself, the broadsheet newspapers, aimed at higher social groups, were

Figure 7: Comparison of baptism *and* christening *used to talk about Christian initiation in newspapers 1995–2015*

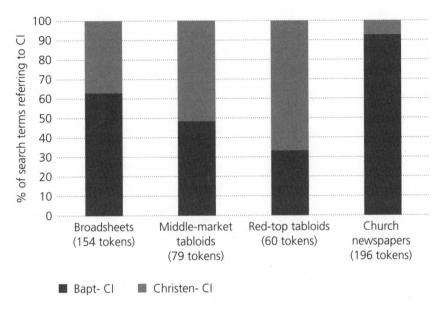

more likely to use *baptism*, the mid-range tabloids were about half and half, and the red-top tabloids, aimed at working-class people, were more likely to use *christening*. In this context, the near total avoidance of *christening* seen in the church newspapers appears in a new light, potentially being interpreted as social snobbery by the working people of the UK. Church language could be seen by some as an extreme version of the language of the social elite.

The split between the language of regular churchgoers and non-churchgoers is seen perhaps most clearly in the study of social media messages posted on Twitter in England (2013–16). This divide between church-based and secular language (Figures 8 and 9) is the starkest of all genres and in all time periods. Twitter messages that had no church connections used *christening* 90 per cent of the time these words were used. Meanwhile church-based messages used *baptism* 96 per cent of the time. As is so often the case, the internet serves to accentuate difference.

Having observed a movement away from the use of *christening* among the general population between the eighteenth and twentieth centuries, does this represent a shift back towards *christening* in the twenty-first century, or is there something about the informality of Twitter that lends itself to an increased use of *christening*? Perhaps a bit of both; this is more extreme than even the language of the *Sun* in the newspaper study cover-

Figure 8: Twitter messages without any clear church connections (total 136 tokens)

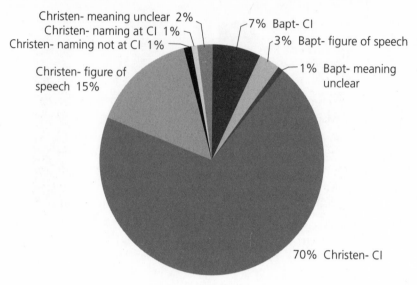

Christen- meaning unclear 2%
Christen- naming at CI 1%
Christen- naming not at CI 1%

7% Bapt- CI
3% Bapt- figure of speech

Christen- figure of
speech 15%

1% Bapt- meaning
unclear

70% Christen- CI

Figure 9: Twitter messages with clear church connections (total 25 tokens)

Christen- CI 4%

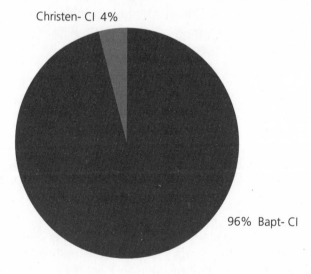

96% Bapt- CI

ing the same time period. But, as Figure 4 shows, even in the most formal and socially elite setting of the Houses of Parliament, *christening* makes a comeback in the late twentieth century. It seems that those people who suggested that *baptism* feels old-fashioned were right, and it is perhaps unsurprising that the Life Events study found that younger people were more likely than older ones to prefer the word *christening*.[24]

Conclusions and overview

What is clear is that clergy and church contexts have continued, throughout the twentieth and twenty-first centuries, to avoid using *christening*, but that this word appears to be making something of a comeback in secular contexts after hundreds of years of decline. The balance between these two types of word varies in the different registers and genres. Overall, a picture has emerged of an increase in the use of *baptism* from the eighteenth century up until the late twentieth century, followed by an increase in the use of *christening* over the turn of the millennium. This is not surprising given the tendency for there to be an increase in informality in language in the late twentieth and early twenty-first centuries.

There are clearly very different patterns of language at different points in history and in different genres, and most tellingly there is a very clear difference in language between clergy/church-based language and lay/secular language throughout all time periods. However, is this theologically significant? Deeper analysis of particular aspects of this language in the following chapters will argue that these linguistic differences, which are difficult for a native speaker to notice in everyday speech and writing, mask significant differences of understandings of the nature of the rite of baptism and what it means to be a Christian.

The extremely strong preference in church-based language for *baptism* is especially significant given the difference in semantic prosody of the two words. These differences in language use reveal something about the attitude that clergy and regular churchgoers have had over the years to baptism. If *christening* is strongly associated with the practical, social and celebratory sides of this rite, then the discomfort of clergy and churchgoers with these words could be seen to reveal a discomfort with a view of baptism that seeks to use it for anything other than religious purposes. This approach to christening is suspicious of the social uses of the rite described in the chapters that follow. This is the view of baptism that corresponds most closely to a congregational or sectarian ecclesiology, in which the Church is seen as a body of religious believers, having clear boundaries and only including those of orthodox belief and practice. Five years ago, when the Life Events team began to present their findings to dioceses and to use the word *christening* in all their outward-facing literature and websites, they found that some clergy were horrified and offended by the use of this word. However, I suspect that resistance among clergy to the use of *christening* is not what it was five years ago, even though *baptism* is still much more widely used in the Church. It would be interesting, in a few years, to extend this study to see if the campaign of the Life Events team has had an impact on the use of language in church-based circles. Certainly, I am not finding the same antipathy to the word that I did when I began my research in 2013.

Those who are not regular churchgoers, but feel some sense of belonging to the Church, tend mainly to see this rite as a *christening*. For some people, *baptism* is likely to sound strange, perhaps rather stuffy and old-fashioned. These people have an attitude to the rite that is reflected in the associations people have with the word *christening*. This attitude sees a christening as a celebratory occasion, with strong social meanings, shown in its connection with social practices such as parties, gifts and the giving of godparents. A christening is an occasion that has deep meanings, confirming a person's identity and name, family and place in society, as they ask for God's blessing on the child and the family, and an intention that he or she should grow up in a loving, broadly Christian setting. This approach to christening is consistent with the societal or church-type ecclesiology. According to this view, the Church is seen as the institution that holds together and celebrates society, and includes all people (in the modern world, this means all those who wish to be included). It is an approach to religion that sees it as the setting in which all of life, the social, the practical, the economic, the emotional, as well as the spiritual, is lived.

By avoiding *christening*, clergy and churchgoers are not only likely to find their language sounds strange to non-churchgoers but also that they miss out on a richer view of baptism, which touches all areas of life. Their exclusive use of *baptism* contributes to a view of this rite that is limited to a narrow, logocentric religiosity. The Church is the inheritor of a rich theological and liturgical tradition, which gives the practice of christening a range of meanings, associations, imagery and symbolism. This inheritance will not be able to make an impact upon those who see themselves as Christian unless it is allowed to be placed within the richer tapestry of the whole of life, including the social and emotional roles of a christening in the lives of ordinary people. The ideal, from the point of view of a rounded and full Christian faith, is for the celebration of this rite to include the meanings contained in both words, *baptism* and *christening*, and so touch all areas of life, as faith in God should ideally do.

Notes

1 Lerer, S. (2007), *Inventing English: A Portable History of the Language*, New York: Columbia University Press, p. 14.

2 Nevalainen, T. (2000), 'Early Modern English Lexis and Semantics', in R. Lass (ed.), *The Cambridge History of the English Language*, Cambridge: Cambridge University Press, p. 332.

3 Minkova, D. and Stockwell, R. (2009), *English Words: History and Structure*, 2nd edn, Cambridge: Cambridge University Press, pp. 205, 207.

4 Minkova and Stockwell (2009), *English Words*, p. 43.

5 Nevalainen (2000), 'Early Modern', p. 332.

6 Corson, D. (1985), *The Lexical Bar*, Oxford: Pergamon.

7 Wycliffe, J., Tyndale, W., Bosworth, J. and Waring, G. (1888), *The Gothic and Anglo-Saxon Gospels in Parallel Columns with the Versions of Wycliffe and Tyndale; Arranged, with Preface and Notes*, London: Reeves & Turner, p. 11. With this and all future quotations from Middle English and Early Modern English, spellings have been updated for ease of reading. Key words are emphasized in bold, with original spellings given afterwards in brackets.

8 *A commentary in Englyshe vpon Sayncte Paules Epystle to the Ephesyans for the instruccyon of them that be vnlerned in tonges*, Early English Books Online.

9 Graph created using the Humanities Digital Workshop at Washington University in St Louis EEBO n-gram tool, which can be found at http://earlyprint.wustl. edu/. The full list of spellings and codes for the parts of speech searched for are listed at the top of the graph, and the graph is smoothed to make trends over time more clear (the raw results are shown more faintly in the background).

10 Figure 2 comes from a combination of searches in this time period in Helsinki Corpus (HC), Parsed Corpus of Early English Correpondence (PCEEC) and Corpus of English Dialogues (CED). See Appendix 2 for details of corpora in this study. In all figures included in this book, CI is used as an abbreviation of Christian Initiation, in order to show clearly when the idea of baptism is being talked about without confusion with the words being studied.

11 *An apology or defence for the Christians of Frau[n]ce which are of the eua[n] gelicall or reformed religion*, Early English Books Online.

12 McGuire, M. B. (2008), *Lived Religion: Faith and Practice in Everyday Life*, Oxford: Oxford University Press, p. 200.

13 Available in Lawrence, S. (2018), 'An Exploration into the Language of Baptism and Christening in the Church of England: A Rite on the Boundaries of the Church', PhD thesis, University of Birmingham, pp. 146, 147.

14 Lawrence (2018), 'An Exploration', p. 111.

15 *Ordinary's Accounts*, Old Bailey Proceedings Online, OA17700419.

16 Joyce, P. (1991), 'The People's English: Language and Class in England c. 1840–1920', in P. Burke and R. Porter (eds), *Language, Self, and Society: A Social History of Language*, Cambridge: Polity, p. 158.

17 This is a linguistic pattern that has been observed, for example, in Labov, W. (1990), 'The Intersection of Sex and Social Class in the Course of Linguistic Change', *Language Variation and Change* 2, p. 205.

18 Cromie, R. and Grose, F. (eds) (1811), *1811 Dictionary of the Vulgar Tongue: A dictionary of buckish slang, university wit and pickpocket eloquence unabridged*

from the original 1811 edition with a foreword by Robert Cromie, Northfield: Digest Books.

19 Half-baptism is a practice mentioned in novels by Dickens in the 1830s, as noted in the *Oxford English Dictionary* entry for 'half-baptize', which is given a primary meaning of 'to baptize privately or without full rites, as a child in danger of death', and a secondary meaning of 'semi-barbarous' or 'deficient in intelligence'. The final example given in the *Oxford English Dictionary* for this is in 1875, in W. D. Parish's 'Dictionary of the Sussex Dialect', OED Online (2016), *Oxford English Dictionary*, Oxford University Press. Retrieved 23.1.17, from www.oed.com.

20 Old Bailey Proceedings Online, t17931030-27.

21 Hansard, HL Deb, 28 March 1963, vol. 248, cc265–322: HOUSE OF LORDS REFORM.

22 Hansard, HL Deb, 25 May 1989, vol. 508, cc572–82: CONTROL OF POLLUTION BILL.

23 Lawrence (2018), 'An Exploration', Appendix 10.

24 Millar, S. (2018), *Life Events: Mission and Ministry at Baptisms, Weddings and Funerals*, London: Church House Publishing, p. 30.

4

Christening, baptism and the giving of a name

The problem with naming at baptism

Many speakers of modern British English see the prime meaning of the word *christening* to be the giving of a name, either to a person at the rite of baptism or to a person or thing at any other time, and indeed this is the first definition of the verb to *christen* in the *Oxford English Dictionary*. However, as demonstrated in Chapter 3, the giving of a name is very much a later addition to a word that originally meant both a Christian person and to baptize someone, that is, to make them a Christian. This is not well understood, and the confusion has led to another source of conflict and misunderstanding between the Church and non-churchgoers who come to seek a christening for their child.

This misunderstanding about the primary meaning of *christening* is important because, if we assume that naming came first, and is a purely secular matter that has become erroneously attached to baptism, then it feels very much like a secular takeover of a sacred rite. If, as is in fact the case, becoming a Christian is the primary meaning, and this extended to the rite of baptism and only very much later to the giving of a name, then we see that naming comes out of the new identity that is gained at baptism and ought to be valued as a marker of Christian identity.

Some people have suggested to me that the phrase *Christian name* came first and that *christened* is a derivative of this. Some argued along the lines that, since a child has traditionally been named at the rite of baptism, the primary meaning for the word *christening* (which they assume to be the giving of a name) came over time to extend to the rite of initiation itself. This assumption has become so common in English folk-linguistics that the misconception is even found among academic writers, as seen in Grimes's investigation into birth rituals: 'The English rite of infant baptism was not only mystical, effecting (but not determining) the divine economy of salvation, but also social. It was the public initiation and naming of a Christian, hence the unofficial title, christening.'[1]

Many theologians and Church historians, when talking about the history of baptism, have taken it for granted that the association between naming and this rite was a popular misconception, a dangerous distraction from its true meaning. 'The folk religion aspect of baptism has always bulked large. In the eighteenth and early nineteenth centuries it was seen by many laity and not a few clergy as a naming ceremony.'[2] Fisher traced the popular association in English culture between baptism and naming to the Book of Common Prayer's command to parents to 'name this child' immediately before the baptism itself. In pre-Reformation services, he tells us, the naming had occurred at a separate stage of the ceremony at the church door, thus making the separation clear. He denounced the decision to move this to the moment of baptism itself at the font as the thing 'which has done most to encourage among the ignorant the notion that baptism is primarily a naming ceremony, and that "to christen" means, chiefly if not entirely, "to name"'.[3]

It seems to have become a matter of doctrine that naming is purely a secular and practical matter, and should not be confused with the important, spiritual, matters with which the Church is concerned. Buchanan, whose work has done much to promote a renewed appreciation for the rite in the Church of England in the latter part of the twentieth century, nevertheless argues that, not only baptism,[4] but even Thanksgiving services, should be clearly disassociated from naming to be sure that there is no confusion; naming occurs when a child is registered, not at church.

> There are churches where the child is solemnly 'named' at a Thanksgiving service. This is not needed and may be misleading. Parents give the child a name at birth, and register the name accordingly – usually long before special church services.[5]

Naming and christening in popular culture

Despite 50 or more years of clergy and theologians arguing that naming should be seen as entirely unconnected with baptism, yet the association continues to exist strongly in the popular imagination. Many portrayals of the rite in film and television focus strongly on naming as a key part of a christening. The 1989 *A Bit of Fry and Laurie* sketch, 'Christening', was entirely about what name to give the child. It opened with the phrase 'I baptize thee Rupert Jeremy James', with the verb *baptize* clearly being used as a synonym of 'named'. When they changed their mind about the name of the child, the vicar objected that he'd just 'done it', and it can't be undone: 'This is a Holy Sacrament of the Church, not a bleeding hotel reservation, you can't just undo it.'[6]

Similarly, in 1991, a christening in an episode of *Only Fools and Horses* focused strongly on the naming, with much of the rest of the service going on in the background while the characters whispered to each other. The vicar's words only came into focus on a couple of occasions, one of which was the naming of the child, which was done by the godfather, as in the traditional formula required in the Book of Common Prayer.[7]

More recently, an episode of the children's cartoon *Horrid Henry* features the christening of Henry's cousin Vera. The vicar is shown saying only '... and I name this baby ...'.[8] Everything else he says in the service is simply shown as mumbling in the background. This clearly shows that, for the makers of this programme, the service is about naming, and everything else is irrelevant background noise. There is no image of water being poured on the baby in this episode, implying that the naming was more significant than the water in the service from the point of view of the cartoon's creators. So, the link between baptism and naming is strong in the popular imagination, but disapproved of by many clergy and theologians. But how far back does the link between christening and naming go, and have clergy always objected to it?

Naming and baptism in the history of the Church

There is little evidence of renaming at baptism in the New Testament. Saul's renaming to Paul occurred considerably after his baptism in the book of Acts, and other renamings in the New Testament are not linked to baptism. Evidence from Roman burial grounds from the early centuries of the Church show that Christian names differed little from their pagan counterparts. However, as more and more infants were baptized, it is likely that parents began, gradually from the third century onwards, to make a connection between the rite and the giving of a name. This was not formally integrated into the ritual, however, until the early Middle Ages.

> Originally, of course, baptism was not a naming ritual, though it does seem that naming was incorporated into the ritual perhaps as early as the eleventh century in parts of the Continent and from the early thirteenth century in English dioceses.[9]

As outlined in Chapter 3, *christened* was commonly used as a verb to refer to the rite of Christian initiation, as well as a noun or adjective to mean 'Christian', in Old English and Middle English. However, I have found only a few examples of its use to mean 'named' before the seventeenth century. The *Oxford English Dictionary* gives Henry Benjamin Wheatley's 'Merlin' as the first example of the use of *christened* to mean named, in about 1450, but this use was clearly a new extension of its main meaning of 'baptized', rather than a primary meaning, and this kind of use was not common in Middle English or Early Modern English.

Until the mid-sixteenth century, *christen* was often used where modern English speakers would use the word *Christian*. Although *christen name* did occur fairly regularly in the texts, it was not used in the same way modern speakers would use *Christian name*, but rather to mean being named as a Christian. Being named as a Christian was a significant idea in pre- and post-Reformation England; much more so than the personal name given at baptism, although these two ideas were closely bound together, as seen in this mid-sixteenth century text:

> and he sayeth that these works do in a **christen** person make the garment of the new man, which garment verily whosoever in the dreadful day of judgement, shall be found under a **christen name** not to have, shall be forthwith taken and cast into utter darkness. (Taverner, 1542)[10]

A person's *christen name* is the honour and responsibility that goes with being named a Christian. This involved being given a personal name, and occasionally *christened* is used in this way to refer to this name, in much the same way modern speakers use the phrase *Christian name*, but this was not the primary use in the fifteenth and sixteenth centuries. The giving of a name before and immediately after the Reformation was not simply a practical matter by which to identify people and remove confusion, but a spiritual act by which a person is identified with Christ at baptism; it is inextricably linked with the salvation that is given and received at the sacrament.

> think upon the great goodness of God how much grace he hath wrought for ye, first in making thee of nought, and then how he with his precious blood bought thee. Departing and discerning thee from all misbelieving people, pagans, and heretics. Giving thee a **christen** name, by receiving of the sacrament of baptism. (Anon, 1535)[11]

In the seventeenth century we begin to see a few more uses of *christened* to mean 'named'. Interestingly, in this time of change and linguistic, as well as religious, innovation, the bloom in uses of *christened* to mean 'named at baptism' occurs at much the same time as a bloom in its use in an allegorical sense to refer to naming, often nicknaming, of people or objects. It is perhaps surprising that *christened* was used to mean named in such a solemn and significant way in the sixteenth century (as seen in the quotation above), and then proceeded so quickly in the seventeenth century to be used in such a jovial, almost frivolous, way, as seen in quotations below.

> A pox on him, he hath **christened** me with a new nickname of Sir Robert Tosspot, that will not part from me this twelvemonth. (Nash, 1600)[12]

> We hear the King is still at Newmarket somewhat troubled with an humour in his great toe which must not yet be **christened** or called the gout. (John Chamberlain, 1613, letter to Ralph Winwood)[13]

At this stage, naming is referred to as *christening* rather than *baptism*. This is perhaps because, in the sixteenth century, it was rare for *baptism* to be used to talk about the rite in practice at all; *baptism* was used to talk about the idea or the theology of baptism, but *christening* to talk about what actually happened in the real world. Hence, in the seventeenth century, the latter extended its meaning to refer to naming, while the former did not until the eighteenth century. One of the first such uses was found in a trial at the Old Bailey: 'I was at the **christening**, and stood godfather; it was **baptized** by the name of William Gardiner' (Mr Cooper, 1740, a witness in the trial of Thomas Hurnell, Bigamy).[14]

By the end of the eighteenth century, though, both *baptism* and *christening* were used to refer to naming, and naming was seen as an increasingly formalized, legal and utilitarian matter; it became this-worldly rather than other-worldly, as it had been in the sixteenth century. As the thinking of the Enlightenment began to influence the culture, sacrality began to diminish in importance. Meanwhile, practical issues, such as the legal status of names, became more important. In the eighteenth century, the Old Bailey trials began to show an increasing concern with the question of how to prove a person's name and identity.

> he came for prize-money due to Patrick How; I asked the prisoner what his name was, he said Dennis Dempsey; I asked him what relation he was to Patrick How, he said he was his half brother ... he said if I had any doubts, he had some other proof; he produced two certificates, one of his own **baptism**, and the other of Patrick How. (Richard Smith, 1807, hospital clerk and witness at the trial of Dennis Dempsey for deception)[15]

References to registers of christenings occurred sporadically in these trials in the eighteenth century (there were seven mentions of registers or certificates of baptism/christenings in 1711–80 in the Old Bailey trials), but this leaped up to a major interest in the early nineteenth century (37 mentions of registers or certificates from 1781 to 1850), remaining high thereafter until the end of the records in 1913 (42 mentions of baptismal certificates or registers from 1850 to 1913). However, with an increased emphasis on the importance of these records came increasing problems over their accuracy, due to clerks' errors, missing records and also with the fact that not all people who were born were christened, for example children of Jewish, Quaker or Baptist families. In addition to this, christening did not always occur within a few weeks of birth, making proof of age uncertain.

The problems with the reliability of these registers led Parliament to seek a secular solution to the problem of establishing a person's name and identity in the early nineteenth century. In 1836 the Registrations Act was passed, providing for a civil registration of births. This led to much concern from various quarters, especially among churchmen, because it was feared that people would register their children instead of baptizing them, as it was assumed that many people used christening merely as a means of registering a child's birth and name.

Now the complaint that he (Mr. Goulburn) made of this arrangement was, that its tendency would be to dissociate the naming of the child from the **baptism**, and in the case of ignorant persons it would induce them to withhold the inestimable benefit of that rite from their children. (Mr Goulburn, 1836, House of Commons)[16]

the Registrars had actually discouraged the **baptism** of children. It was intimated, that it was not necessary that **baptism** should take place immediately; the consequence was, that it was delayed from week to week, from month to month, from year to year, and so the children never got **baptised** at all. He complained, that the registration of the births of children by the Church, had not been left undisturbed. (The Bishop of London, 1839, House of Lords)[17]

Cases in Old Bailey trial records about the deaths or abduction of infants usually would not give the child's name unless he or she had been baptized. Sometimes the parents would informally use a name for the child, as seen in the first quotation below (in this case the name was acknowledged by the court), but other times no name was mentioned at all, as seen in the case of the 8-week-old baby in the second quotation. This leads to a dehumanizing effect to modern ears, in the way the baby is talked about as 'it' and without a name.

> CATHARINE CRAWLEY. I am single. I had a child living – it was a girl; it would be six months old, this month – its name was Mary Moore; I do not know that it had been **baptized** – I called it Mary Moore. (1828, trial of Margaret Hartigan for murder)[18]

> I had been searching for the child all the day and all the night – it was very ill when it came back – it has been in fits ever since – I took it to the doctor – it is a male child – it was not **christened**. (Elizabeth Purdy, 1844, trial of Amelia Smith and Eleanor Stanton for kidnapping)[19]

After the Act of Registration in 1838 there is some evidence that registration was considered sufficient to establish a name. However, without baptism many still felt that the name was of doubtful validity. This was seen in the 1842 trial of Mary Ann Dunn for kidnapping.

> I was in a public-house in seven Dials, with my infant – it was then three weeks and two days old – it was registered – it had not been **christened** – it was called joseph Dawes. (Harriet Dawes, 1842, trial of Mary Ann Dunn for kidnapping)[20]

> I am master of Croydon workhouse. On Thursday afternoon, the 31st of March, the officer brought the prisoner there with the child ... I asked her what name I should put down – was it **christened**? – she said it was no name. (Mr. Hale, 1842, trial of Mary Ann Dunn for kidnapping)[21]

This doubt as to whether an unbaptized person could really be considered to have a name persisted into the twentieth century for some people.

> I beg to ask the Secretary of State for the Home Department whether he is aware that the rector of Irthlingborough, Northamptonshire, has refused to publish the banns of marriage between Mr. Arthur J. Bayes and Miss Wimhurst, on the ground that the former has not been **baptised**, and, therefore, has no Christian name. (Mr Channing, 1902, House of Commons)[22]

This kind of debate about whether naming was possible without baptism was even seen as late as the 1950s, with debates over identity cards in the House of Lords.

The noble Lord, Lord Mancroft, spoke of a baby who could not have an identity card until it had been **baptised**. What the writer in the Daily Mail said was: The vicar refused to **christen** the child until its identity card had been produced. The parents contended that it could not have a card until it had a name. Actually, a baby can have an identity card as soon as its birth has been registered, and its birth can be registered before it has been **christened**. (Lord Shepherd, 1951, House of Lords)[23]

While this was clearly no longer a legal debate by this point in the mid-twentieth century, and was perhaps a concern for only a minority of people, yet the possibility that naming could be seen as impossible without baptism persisted for well over a hundred years after the Act of Registration. Moreover, christening did not cease to be sought by parents, as feared by Mr Goulburn in the House of Commons in 1836 and by the Bishop of London in the House of Lords in 1839; baptism was in fact still very popular at the start of the twentieth century. People wanted a christening for more reasons than simply to register legally their child's birth. Naming was still a foundational part of what parents sought in presenting their children for baptism, but this was not conceived of as a merely practical or legal matter.

The use of *christening* and *baptism* to refer to naming was a known but not common use of these words in the texts that I studied from the seventeenth to the nineteenth century. But at the end of the nineteenth century, the use of *christened* to mean figuratively 'named' (e.g. giving a nickname to a thing or person) increased substantially as a proportion of the ways these words were used in speeches in the Houses of Parliament, and from this point on this use remained relatively high. From the late nineteenth to the late twentieth centuries between 5 and 25 per cent of all uses of *christening* in the debates in the Houses of Commons and of Lords referred to figurative naming. Meanwhile, the use of *christened* to refer to naming at baptism, and the use of *baptism* to refer to either type of naming, was relatively low.

This pattern of the use of *christened* to refer figuratively to naming (not at baptism) was common also in the newspaper corpus (1990–2015), with nearly 20 per cent of all uses of *christening* referring to figurative naming in the secular newspapers in my study. However, in other genres of text or speech studied in the late twentieth and early twenty-first centuries, this use of these words was still at a fairly low rate. Less formal and rehearsed genres of speech used this meaning of *christened* much less frequently. In the 1990s, in the spoken element of the British National Corpus, which included many transcripts of conversations, less than 2 per cent of non-church context uses of *christened* referred to figurative naming. In fact, the use of *christened* to refer to naming at baptism was much more common than the figurative use in this corpus, at nearly 7 per cent of all uses.

There is a sense that the use of *christened* to mean 'named' is somewhat colloquial and informal. Indeed, *The Guardian*'s style guide encourages its journalists to avoid this use of *christened*, advising that it should be used 'only when referring to a Christian baptism: don't talk about a boat being christened or a football club christening a new stadium; named is fine'.[24] It is interesting that *The Guardian* journalists pay very little heed to this, and in fact use it even more than other newspapers, including most of the tabloid newspapers, with 32 per cent of all uses of *christening* in the samples of texts taken from *The Guardian* from 1995 to 2015 referring to naming, either at baptism or figuratively. Far from being a colloquial use, this study has shown that it is texts (spoken or written) that have been carefully crafted to impress their audience that use the figurative sense of *christened* much more than in natural speech, leading to many witty rhetorical flourishes in the Houses of Parliament such as these:

> Mr. REMER asked the President of the Board of Trade whether he is aware that the Japanese have **christened** a village in Japan 'Macclesfield,' in order to enable them to sell their silk goods as Macclesfield silk; and whether he will take the appropriate steps to prevent these goods being sold in the home market marked in this way;
> Mr. SORENSEN: Can the hon. Member say whether, in fact, they **christen** at all in Japan? (1936, House of Commons)[25]

> The position under this Bill is that the local licensing authorities are re-**christened**; the Traffic Commissioners are re-**christened**; the licensing authority for public service vehicles and the regional authorities under the Act of 1933 are re-**christened** licensing authorities. I have no objection to these **baptismal** regenerations. What matters is not the name but the powers. (Viscount Swinton, 1947, House of Lords).[26]

Is naming a spiritual or purely secular matter in the twenty-first century?

Clergy's concerns about the 1836 Registration Act were deeply felt; there was a sense among clergy of the nineteenth century that it was vital for baptism to remain linked with naming in the popular imagination.

However, they were concerned in this loss mainly with the anticipated reduction in the numbers of people presenting their children for baptism and the loss of power and influence of the Church if it was no longer to be the keeper of official records of people's names and ages. They showed a complete lack of concern that naming itself should be a spiritual and not just a practical matter. This idea appears to have been lost well before 1836.

Occasionally, however, the underlying spiritual significance of naming comes to the fore, even in the twenty-first century. In 2015, the Revd Chris Newlands caused a media storm when he offered a service of reaffirmation of baptismal vows to a transgender man, who had approached him and asked to be re-baptized. Newlands explained that this was not possible; but when he asked why he wanted this, he answered as follows: 'he was originally baptized as a baby girl, and to him it was about God knowing him by name. He was no longer the little girl he was baptized as.'[27] It is interesting to note that, despite some concern among some people about the misuse of baptismal rites for renaming of transgender people, the House of Bishops' advice on a service to mark gender transition is to use baptism or a reaffirmation of baptismal vows:

> The emphasis is placed not on the past or future of the candidate alone, but on their faith in Jesus Christ. The Affirmation therefore gives priority to the original and authentic baptism of the individual as the sacramental beginning of the Christian life, allowing someone who has undergone a serious and lasting change to re-dedicate their life and identity to Christ. The image of God, in which we are all made, transcends gender, race, and any other characteristic.[28]

Names are hugely significant for a person's identity, not only as an individual but within society. Naming is a fundamentally important ideological action, in which the family's values and identity are interpolated in the naming process and passed on to the child. A name 'defines an individual's position in his family and in society at large; it defines his social personality'.[29]

Names can make clear a person's family and cultural heritage, and often show their religious heritage. Names give people social clues about a person's race, class and ethnicity, and usually, though not always, will make the child's gender clear. This use of names to define people has been used, in both positive and negative ways, throughout history. In Nazi Germany, Aryans were required to choose names from a list of approved, racially appropriate names, while Jewish parents were required to add 'Israel' or 'Sarah' to their names, to make their ethnicity clear.[30]

There is strong evidence that a person's name has a significant impact on many aspects of their life. It has been shown to affect a person's chances of getting a job. It can impact upon assumptions people make about a person's age, gender, ethnic and social grouping and even intellectual competence and attractiveness. By naming a child, parents are not only marking them as an individual but also placing them within the social system, adopting them into the group and acknowledging them as 'one of us'. Naming has a deep significance for parents as they bond with their child, even before birth. In cases of stillbirth, it has been shown that naming can be helpful for parents to 'talk to and about their babies and hence recognize them as persons'.[31] Naming, and how a person feels about their name, is also closely linked with self-esteem and identity.

This is not merely a practical matter, or even merely a secular one. It has deep spiritual significance for which there is a precedent in Christian thought, as argued above. This sense of recognizing an individual and adopting them into a group is exactly what happens at baptism: a person is being adopted into the Church; they are being recognized and made into a Christian; they are taking on a new identity; they become a new creation in the eyes of God and the Christian community.

> for in Christ Jesus you are all children of God through faith. As many of you as were baptized into Christ have clothed yourselves with Christ. There is no longer Jew or Greek, there is no longer slave or free, there is no longer male and female; for all of you are one in Christ Jesus. And if you belong to Christ, then you are Abraham's offspring, heirs according to the promise. (Galatians 3.26–29)

At baptism, St Paul argues, a person changes their identity from their natural inheritance of nationality, status or gender, and are adopted into the family of Christ. This strong link between identity and naming is behind the common practice of name changes on conversion in many religions, and behind the practice of taking on a new name when a person makes monastic vows in some Christian and Buddhist traditions. Name changes have had religious significance for millennia, as seen in the frequency of name changes for biblical characters, both in the Old and New Testaments (e.g. Genesis 17.5, 15; John 1.42), reflecting changing status or relationship with God (even though, as noted above, these name changes do not seem to be associated with baptism).

In the pre-Reformation Church, the choice of names itself was seen as a significant part of this adoption into the community of the Church, with various conventions existing at different points in time and place over choices of names. Overall, there was a concern that names reflected

Christian values and stories. Archbishop Pecham of Canterbury gave orders, in the late thirteenth century, to clergy to ensure that children were not given 'improper' names.[32] And in the twenty-first century this continues to be a concern, as seen in Pope Benedict XVI's 2011 statement praising the importance of a 'Christian name',[33] which was widely reported in the media as an attack on the rise of popular secular names.[34]

There is an irony in the tendency of names given at a christening to mark an individual as belonging to a particular culture, class, nation or family group. According to St Paul, baptism marks an individual as belonging to God, and thus erases the differences that are so important in ordinary social life. In St Paul's world, these social differences were characterized as Jew or Greek, slave or free, male or female. In our world, the latter of these is still relevant (and sometimes problematic, as seen in the case of the transgender man discussed above), but the former two sets may be regarded as equivalent to differences of class, social level and race. The irony is that these are the very things that naming tends to differentiate people by and emphasize. The attachment of a name to a person when they are christened can mark them as a Christian by giving them a name from the Christian tradition, thus declaring their Christian background to others. Yet this Christian identity can, in itself, become a tribal identity as much as a spiritual allegiance to Christ, and so naming at baptism can be seen as not unproblematic.

Christianity is an incarnational religion: it is based upon the belief that God chose to become a human being, and he did this at a particular time in history, in a particular ethnic and religious group, in a particular family, in a particular body, at a particular time. Jesus was named with a name that was common in his culture, which would have marked him to all as male, as Jewish, as coming from Israel, a nation under the occupation of the Roman Empire. This scandal of particularity makes Paul's statement, that in Christ there is no Jew or Greek, slave or free, male or female, somewhat problematic. Jesus was male. Jesus was free, but not a Roman citizen. Jesus was self-consciously Jewish and regarded himself as being sent 'to the lost sheep of the house of Israel' (Matthew 15.24). Jesus came to the particular, and from the particular he transformed the universal. He began in a human family, society, race, religion and nation.

For the followers of Jesus, baptism marks the beginning of a journey, which starts from the particular and leads beyond this to a vision of all humanity united under one God. For this reason, the giving of a name at baptism is appropriate, as Christians are acknowledged by the community and by God as they are, in the body, family and community in which they are found. Naming recognizes this and affirms people before

God. This is the starting point from which a Christian journey, which may transcend the social realities of gender, race and class, may begin.

Imposing names and imposing religion on babies at baptism

The debate about whether it is appropriate to impose a religion on a child by administering baptism shortly after birth applies equally to naming. Is it right to impose a gender identity on a child who may at a later stage feel they do not rightly belong to that gender? Is it right to impose a name on a child that makes their ethnic background clear, and distinguishes them from people of other cultures? Is it right to impose a name on a child that makes clear their inheritance of a particular faith, which they may at a later stage in life choose to reject and/or change to a different religion? Perhaps children should be allowed to choose their own name when they reach maturity? But, does that make a child a non-person until they are adults, existing only on a provisional basis to be confirmed at a later date?

A person who chooses to change their country, culture or religion will always be shaped by the inheritance they had in their upbringing; they will always be an immigrant in the new location or a convert in the new faith. This, then, becomes part of their new identity; it is not removed in the change, even if they choose to change their name to reflect their new identity. Parents, family and the community in which a child grows up do shape a child, they do make choices for them, and these continue to be significant even when that child chooses to change direction later in life. It is a profound thing to name a child, and a solemn recognition of this seems appropriate in some ritual action. I would argue that baptism can be an appropriate ritual action in which a child can be given a name, although other ritual actions may also be appropriate. The use of the baptism service, or the reaffirmation of baptismal vows, to acknowledge a new name and identity before God for transgender people is also a good use of these rites.

To be known by name to God, as the man who approached the Revd Chris Newlands to request re-baptism knew, is a profound experience of being known, of being seen and recognized by God. This sense of dwelling in the divine gaze is something that christening can offer a person, and it is often overlooked. To be given a name before God carries multiple levels of meaning at baptism. It recognizes the candidate as an individual, but also as a member of a family, a community and the Christian faith. It 'informs' God of this new name, so that the candidate can be assured that God knows him or her, and it also 'informs' the community of the new name, so that they also can recognize and celebrate this person as an individual within the family and community.

As the catechism makes clear, promises are made in a person's name at baptism: that the person will endeavour to live up to the responsibilities that will be placed upon him or her as a Christian. This is more controversial. Surely it is unreasonable to place upon an infant the responsibility to keep promises made in their name, which they themselves did not know they were agreeing to? This was not a problem to the mind of the seventeenth century, as the catechism makes clear:

> *Question.* What did your Godfathers and Godmothers then for you?
> *Answer.* They did promise and vow three things **in my name**. First, that I should renounce the devil and all his works ... Secondly, that I should believe all the articles of the Christian faith. And thirdly, that I should keep God's holy will and commandments, and walk in the same all the days of my life.
> *Question.* Dost thou not think that thou art bound to believe, and to do, as they have promised for thee?
> *Answer.* Yes verily: and by God's help so I will. And I heartily thank our heavenly Father, that he hath called me to this state of salvation, through Jesus Christ our Saviour. And I pray unto God to give me his grace, that I may continue in the same unto my life's end.[35]

In the seventeenth century, it was seen (by the Church at least) as an honour and a joy to live up to the promises made in one's name at one's christening. In the twenty-first century, however, in an era that values personal choice and freedom over most other virtues, this is an increasingly difficult idea.

Nevertheless, we do have expectations of the children who grow up in our society: that they should keep the laws and accept punishment if they do not, that they should treat others with respect, courtesy and toleration, that they should abide by certain behavioural expectations. While the promises made on a child's behalf at baptism would no longer be considered something to hold them to by force, as it would have been in the seventeenth century, yet the idea of setting out expectations and boundaries within which parents aim to bring up their children, including religious expectations, does not seem an unreasonable starting place to provide a strong religious identity for the child, a starting place for a path on which they may choose to continue or move on from.

Recommendations for pastoral practice

Few people in English society today would christen a child and see it as a commitment that the child must keep and be punished if they do not; most people would see it as the child's right to change their religion later on, if they so choose. Perhaps this emphasis on personal choice will lead infant baptism to become obsolete in the near future; certainly, the numbers have declined sharply in the latter part of the twentieth and the early part of the twenty-first centuries. However, there is still a need to resolve the liminality of children, to transition them from being 'not a person' to being a member of society, of a family, and to being an individual. There is a need to transition them into the rights and respon-sibilities of their community. These important meanings could certainly be contained within a system of naming ceremonies offered to families, and the Church would do well to promote and support the provision of such ceremonies for families who would not otherwise seek a baptism for their children. The service of Thanksgiving for the Gift of a Child would be a good starting place for such a service. However, this service has not been widely sought after by non-church families, mainly because the name of the service is not understood or meaningful to most people. If the service was used under the title of a 'naming ceremony', this may make it much more attractive to families seeking to mark the arrival of a new child to the family in an appropriately solemn way. The Thanksgiv-ing service even has the option for either parents or 'supporting friends' to name the child, echoing the role of godparents in the 1662 baptismal service.[36] This optional aspect of a Thanksgiving service could be given much more emphasis in a church naming ceremony, with family mem-bers being invited to speak about what the name means to them, and/or the vicar talking about the origins and associations of that name as part of the sermon. Small ritual actions could be added, such as the giving of a handprint with the name of the child written on it, accompanied by the quotation from Isaiah 49.16: 'God has written your name on the palms of his hands' (this is an adaptation from the New Living Translation).

However, naming is also theologically significant and closely linked with the Church's traditional understandings of the meanings of baptism: to join a new community, to gain a new identity as an individual under God, to make promises in this name to adhere to the expectations of the faith. The neglect of naming by the Church as a meaning of baptism is a neglect that has impoverished its understanding of the importance of this rite, and left it further removed from the people it is trying to connect with.

Clergy and congregations need to be aware of the pastoral and family significance of naming and not downplay this aspect of baptism in how they conduct the ceremony and care for the families. The Book of Common Prayer had a command that the minister at baptism asks the godparents to 'name this child'.[37] This demand was kept in the proposed 1928 Prayer Book, but by 1980, when the Alternative Service Book was published, this demand was changed to the instruction: 'He dips him in the water or pours water on him, addressing him by name.'[38] By the time the *Common Worship* service of Holy Baptism was published, even this instruction was omitted, and no reference was made to the name at all, except that the name should be used at the time of baptism: 'N, I baptize you in the name of the Father, and of the Son, and of the Holy Spirit.'[39] The 2015 Common Worship resource 'Additional Baptism Texts in Accessible Language' has gone a little way in restoring the importance of naming at a christening. At the 'presentation' of the child towards the start of the service, the vicar addresses the parents and godparents in a way that acknowledges the importance of naming:

God knows each of us by name and we are his.
Parents and godparents, you speak for N and N today.
Will you pray for them,
and help them to follow Christ?
We will.[40]

These changes in the additional texts could have gone further and included the question that is present in the Thanksgiving service, 'What name have you given this child?', as a restoration of the question addressed to godparents in the 1662 baptismal service, which honours the importance of naming to families and before God. It would be particularly appropriate if this question could be addressed to the godparents, recognizing the real role they play in the life of the child and in the family.

The spiritual significance of naming is a key that could make some of the deeper meanings of baptism accessible to non-churchgoers, and it is a theme that ought to be re-embraced by the Church. The name of the child, and God's concern for the child as an individual and for the whole family, would be an appropriate theme for the sermon at a christening. Clergy could also show more interest in the naming of the child when preparing families for baptism. While this is a decision that will have been already made, a conversation about the name chosen and the reasons for the choice would be a helpful point of pastoral contact, and a way in to talk about the meaning of the ritual.

Finally, while parents would undoubtedly resent interference from clergy on what they name their children at the time of baptism, it may be appropriate for clerics to remind their flock occasionally of the importance of names and encourage them to remember their Christian heritage when naming their children.

Notes

1 Grimes, R. L. (2000), *Deeply into the Bone: Re-inventing Rites of Passage*, Berkeley: University of California Press, p. 54.

2 Hinton, M. (1994), *The Anglican Parochial Clergy: A Celebration*, London: SCM Press, p. 254.

3 Fisher, J. D. C. (1965), *Christian Initiation: Baptism in the Medieval West: A Study in the Disintegration of the Primitive Rite of Initiation*, London: SPCK, p. 157.

4 Buchanan, C. (1980), 'Initiation Services', in C. Buchanan, T. Lloyd and H. Miller (eds), *Anglican Worship Today: Collins Illustrated Guide to the Alternative Service Book 1980*, London: Collins, p. 158.

5 Buchanan (1992), *Infant Baptism in the Church of England: A Guide to the Official Position of the Church in its Formularies*, Nottingham: Grove Books, p. 9.

6 BBC (1989), *A Bit of Fry and Laurie*, 'Christening'. Retrieved 8.2.18, from http://abitoffryandlaurie.co.uk/sketches/christening, series 1, episode 5.

7 BBC (1991), *Only Fools and Horses*, 'Damien's Christening, extract from Miami Twice, part 1'. Retrieved 15.12.16, from www.youtube.com/watch?v=Tx65lSHwJFk.

8 Novel Entertainment Ltd (2011), *Horrid Henry and the Christening Crisis*, based on the books by Francesca Simon, illustrated by Tony Ross and published by Orion Books. Retrieved 15.12.16, from www.youtube.com/watch?v=PxWtNBK-Bxs&t=209s.

9 Wilson, S. (1998), *The Means of Naming: A Social and Cultural History of Personal Naming in Western Europe*, London: UCL Press, p. 99.

10 *On Saynt Andrewes day the Gospels with brief sermons vpon them for al the holy dayes in ye yere*, Early English Books Online.

11 *A deuout treatyse called the tree and xii. frutes of the holy goost*, Early English Books Online.

12 *A pleasant comedie, called Summers last will and testament*, Early English Books Online.

13 Parsed Corpus of Early English Correspondence, Chamber, 29.

14 Old Bailey Proceedings, t17400116-45.

15 Old Bailey Proceedings, t18070408-81.

16 Hansard, HC Deb, 6 June 1836, vol. 34 cc130–45: REGISTRATION BILL. – HALF-PAY OFFICERS.

17 Hansard, HL Deb, 5 March 1839, vol. 45 cc1253–61: MARRIAGE ACT.

18 Old Bailey Proceedings, t18280911-16.

19 Old Bailey Proceedings, OBP t18441021-2578a.

20 Old Bailey Proceedings, t18420404-1381.

21 Old Bailey Proceedings, t18420404-1381.

22 Hansard, HC Deb, 25 March 1902, vol. 105 c991.

23 Hansard, HL Deb, 26 July 1951, vol. 172 cc1335–73.

24 *The Guardian* (2016), 'Guardian and Observer Style Guide: C'. Retrieved 21.6.17, from www.theguardian.com/guardian-observer-style-guide-c.

25 Hansard, HC Deb, 25 May 1936, vol. 312 cc1635–6, 1635.

26 Hansard, HL Deb, 19 June 1947, vol. 148 cc1053–155: 'TRANSPORT BILL'.

27 Lakin, N. (2015), 'Church Needs to "Catch Up" as Vicar Urges Gender Debate', *Lancaster Guardian*, 4 June 2015. Retrieved 2.12.15, from www.lancaster guardian.co.uk/news/local/church-needs-to-catch-up-as-vicar-urges-gender-debate-1-7293295#ixzz3tAWgPC53.

28 Church of England (2018), *Pastoral Guidance for Use in Conjunction with the Affirmation of Baptismal Faith in the Context of Gender Transition*. Retrieved 3.7.19, from www.churchofengland.org/sites/default/files/2018-12/Pastoral%20 Guidance-Affirmation-Baptismal-Faith.pdf.

29 Wilson (1998), *The Means of Naming*, p. xii.

30 Jewish Telegraphic Agency (1938), 'Reich Publishes List of "Jewish Names" Barred to "Aryans"'. Retrieved 3.7.17, from www.jta.org/1938/08/24/archive/ reich-publishes-list-of-jewish-names-barred-to-aryans.

31 Aldrin, E. (2016), 'Names and Identity', in C. Hough and D. Izdebska (eds), *The Oxford Handbook of Names and Naming*, Oxford: Oxford University Press, p. 386.

32 Wilson (1998), *The Means of Naming*, p. 99.

33 Pope Benedict XVI (2011), On the Feast of the Baptism of the Lord, St Peter's Square, Rome. Retrieved 16.12.16, from http://w2.vatican.va/content/benedict-xvi/ en/angelus/2011/documents/hf_ben-xvi_ang_20110109_battesimo.html.

34 Squires, N. (2011), 'Pope Rails Against Rise of un-Christian Names', *The Telegraph*. Retrieved 16.12.16, from www.telegraph.co.uk/news/worldnews/the-pope/8251791/Pope-rails-against-rise-of-un-Christian-Names.html.

35 Book of Common Prayer (1662), p. 289, emphasis added.

36 Compare the role of supporting friends in 'Thanksgiving for the Gift of a Child', in Church of England (2006), *Common Worship: Christian Initiation*, London: Church House Publishing, p. 19, with the role of godparents in naming the child in the Book of Common Prayer (1662), 'Publick Baptism of Infants' service, p. 269.

37 Book of Common Prayer, p. 269.

38 Church of England (1980), *The Alternative Service Book 1980, together with The Liturgical Psalter*, London: Hodder & Stoughton, p. 247.

39 Church of England (2006), *Common Worship: Christian Initiation*, p. 71.

40 Archbishops' Council (2015), 'Christian Initiation: Additional Baptism Texts in Accessible Language', London: Church House Publishing. Retrieved 23/4/19, from www.churchofengland.org/prayer-and-worship/worship-texts-and-resources/ common-worship/christian-initiation/christian.

5

Marriage-like vows

When searching through the newspapers, books, letters, court transcripts and other texts in this study, I was expecting to find a strong set of 'folk beliefs' associated with *christening* in the past, but that these would be weakening as the uptake of the rite decreased. I was surprised to find a new meaning emerging in non-church-based texts, from the 1990s onwards. I have called this new meaning 'marriage-like vows' because parents and others began to see the primary point of having a christening as making promises of love and commitment to a child before God and in public, rather like a couple do in a church marriage service.

Marriage-like vows of love and commitment

While searching YouTube to see which videos were associated with the words *baptism* and *christening*, I found the 'Christening Song', and was struck by the very different view of baptism contained in this song compared to that promoted by the Church. The song was like a love song to the children being christened. For those writing the song, christening was not about promising to bring the children up as Christians, or about joining the Church, but about a declaration of commitment and love towards them, which was aiming to carry the children through all that life brings. These vows seem to be the main point of what baptism meant for the godparents who wrote the song for their godchildren, and they struck me as comparable to the vows made at a marriage, which are made to the beloved in the sight of God. This song is far from being purely secular. These promises are made before God, God's blessing is sought for the girls, and prayers are said for them.

> And this is the promise we make
> This is the vow we take
> We'll love you til our hearts ache
> And now onto God we pray
> He'll bless you in every way
> Each day be a happy day for you.[1]

Is this view of baptism a secular abuse of the Church's rite of initiation or a positive, theologically valuable, extension of its meaning? This question will be addressed further at the end of this chapter, once a fuller picture of the prevalence of these marriage-like vows and other social uses of christening have been explored.

Many of the secular sources that I have studied, from the latter part of the twentieth century and early twenty-first century, have expressed an approach to baptism similar to the 'Christening Song': as like a marriage between parents and children, and between godparents and godchildren. The expression of love and commitment towards the child is seen as paramount in the meaning of the ceremony. These are the elements of a christening that have carried over into secular naming ceremonies, which shows that it is these elements of the rite's meaning that have been missed as rates of baptism have fallen, rather than the more overtly religious elements emphasized by the churches. Baptism has been seen as a rite of passage to mark a birth, giving a child a name and recognizing him or her as part of the society and the family since before the Reformation. However, this very overt link between christening and making a formal statement of love towards a child is not made explicit in the sources I have studied prior to the 1990s, but after this it became quite common.

'Our first son was born with lethal disorders, the result of a chromosome abnormality. He lived for only a few days, but long enough to be loved and to be **baptised**' (1990, Robert Key, House of Commons).[2] This quotation shows how the attachment between parents and children, and the use of christening as an expression of this love, began to be seen as an assumed part of what baptism was about at the end of the twentieth century. As the twenty-first century dawned, this expression of love and commitment became a key element of what families sought at a christening and at secular alternatives such as naming ceremonies. This is perhaps partly because society had become more emotionally expressive by this time. But it is likely that it is also a societal response to developments in the field of psychology, which highlighted more and more, through the twentieth century, the importance of secure attachments and love in childhood, if individuals are to grow up to be flourishing adults. This emphasis on the importance of the right kind of parenting for the future life prospects of children has crept into the popular imagination, and many parents have become anxious about providing the right atmosphere of love and support that children need in order to thrive.

At some time of their lives, I believe, most human beings desire to have children and desire also that their children should grow up to be healthy, happy, and self-reliant. For those who succeed the rewards are great;

but for those who have children but fail to rear them to be healthy, happy, and self-reliant the penalties in anxiety, frustration, friction, and perhaps shame or guilt, may be severe. Engaging in parenthood therefore is playing for high stakes. Furthermore, because successful parenting is a principal key to the mental health of the next generation, we need to know all we can both about its nature and about the manifold social and psychological conditions that influence its development for better or worse.[3]

Being loving and attentive and having a good network of support for the parent(s) is seen as particularly important, both by psychologists and in the popular consciousness. The reverse side of this is that failure to provide a secure base is seen as the cause of problems later in life. This led Frank Field MP in 2003 to argue in the House of Commons that antisocial behaviour was linked to the decline in rates of baptism. He wished to bring back some ceremony that would fulfil the role that christening once did, which was seen as building family networks and expressing commitment to take the role of parenting seriously, as well as initiating new children into the wider society:

> For two thirds of children, there is no public ceremony whereby we welcome them into our community and say, 'Welcome. You are now part of something wider than your family.' I therefore hope that the Government will consider making the registration of birth a public ceremony and a public event, in which we as society say, 'Welcome. This is what we are going to provide for you ... and this is the framework within which we expect your parents to operate.' (1990, Frank Field, House of Commons)[4]

An emphasis upon the importance of childhood in understanding the psychological problems that people can develop had been growing since the work of Freud, who thought that neuroses had origins in childhood. This led to a concern for the healthy development of children, especially in the wake of the First World War, in which children were often subject to terrible conditions. In 1924, just six years after Freud published *From the History of an Infantile Neurosis*, the League of Nations issued the Declaration of the Rights of the Child, which stated that all children had a right to various material needs, such as food, shelter, relief from distress, and be given 'the means requisite for its normal development, both materially and spiritually'.[5] This was developed and considerably extended in 1959 by the UN, which issued a new Declaration, which included many new elements, including an emphasis upon love and family life:

The child, for the full and harmonious development of his personality, needs love and understanding. He shall, wherever possible, grow up in the care and under the responsibility of his parents, and, in any case, in an atmosphere of affection and of moral and material security.[6]

In the second half of the twentieth century, there was a growing explicit emphasis upon the importance of love and a secure family environment in childhood for human flourishing. This coincided with the decline in uptake of baptism in the UK, and a decline in churchgoing and allegiance to the Christian faith. It also coincided with a time of increased divorce rates, unmarried and single parents, and new patterns of family life resulting from these social changes. It was in this context that families began to see a christening as an opportunity to make promises of love and commitment to their children, in the light of the anxieties that these social changes brought, and the increased emphasis upon the importance of love for the future flourishing of children. If this began as a subtle new factor influencing parents' decisions to christen their children, over time it became more accepted and normal, and began to be stated overtly as an assumed part of the purpose and meaning of baptism, thus making an appearance in the texts in my study from 1990 onwards.

Naming ceremonies

The proportion of the English population who were baptized as infants fell dramatically over the second half of the twentieth century and the early part of the twenty-first century. This decline has left some people feeling that an important element of the life of families and the nation has been lost, and to seek to rebuild this through offering secular alternatives to baptism, such as naming ceremonies, which fulfil some of the same needs. Frank Field's call for a secular alternative to baptism, noted above, began in 1995, in the following speech in the House of Commons.

I beg to move, 'That leave be given to bring in a Bill to empower registrars of births to conduct civil naming ceremonies ...
As well as celebrating a sacrament, **baptism** was an event to welcome a child into the community ... When the British expeditionary forces set sail in the first world war, practically every person in that contingent would have been **baptised** ... When we went down to the sea in great ships to engage in the Falklands war, only one third of those engaging in that conflict had been **baptised**. (1995, Frank Field, House of Commons)[7]

Baptism has historically, among other uses, acted as a way of incorporating children into society, of placing upon them, at the start of their lives, the expectations that society would have of them. Prior to the mid-twentieth century this was understood as including an expectation that they would follow the Christian faith, in terms of both beliefs and ethics. In return, society made a promise to the children, to bring them up within English society, which included being within the Christian faith. For families, christening offered a chance to officially recognize new children as people, to give them a name, and to incorporate them into a Christian family. The Registration of Births Act (1836) took away some of these functions – the official and bureaucratic elements of them, recording their name, parents, date of birth, etc. – but other elements remained important in the act of baptism, such as the incorporation of the child into the family, into society, and making promises on behalf of the child and to the child. However, in the latter part of the twentieth century, concern was beginning to grow about the huge fall in rates of christenings in England.

At the end of the twentieth century, there was an attempt to regain some of the social functions that had been lost in the demise of baptism. The initial proposal to do this was to make registrations of birth a public ceremony, much like a civil wedding, including promises made to the child, and responsibilities and rights formalized in declarations. This idea was introduced in 1995 by Lord Young of Dartington into the House of Lords, and by Frank Field in the House of Commons. The idea was modified over time to give people the right to request Registrars hold a naming ceremony when they registered the birth. These ceremonies began to be offered by local councils in 2000. For some, this was baptism emptied of its spiritual meaning, and some clergy were concerned that people would mistakenly think that this was a 'christening', and not realize the child had not been baptized.

> My Lords, does the Minister accept that while we on these Benches strongly support all measures to strengthen family life ... we are ... bound to have reservations about a civil naming ceremony which seems to adopt many of the features of Christian **baptism** while emptying them of their spiritual content? Would it not therefore be preferable for the Churches to redouble their efforts to reach out and encourage parents to consider bringing their children to **baptism** rather than adopting a confusingly similar imitation which is deprived of its full spiritual meaning? (1995, Bishop of Lichfield, House of Lords)[8]

Frank Field's main motivation for introducing the measure was the rise in children born to cohabiting couples, together with a perceived rise in the numbers of clergy refusing to christen children, especially those of unmarried parents. There was a concern that the rise in cohabitation would result in more failed families and more children growing up without the support of a traditional nuclear family, leading to social problems in the future.

On many levels, there was a hope that naming ceremonies would perform the role of social cohesion (and maybe also coercion) that baptism used to have. It was intended to make families who may be in danger of bringing up anti-social children aware of the responsibilities society expected of them as parents. In the event, however, naming ceremonies, because they are optional, have only been taken up by those already committed to the importance of family.

Naming ceremonies have become an accepted part of life for many people because it allows them to celebrate a new birth and cement the relationship of the family (both the nuclear and extended family) with the new child by making marriage-like vows to love and care for the child, similar to those noted above in connection with christenings. For such families, naming ceremonies offered many of the important social benefits of baptism without the pretence of a religion that was not really followed or imposing a faith upon a child too young to choose. The quotation below appeared in the *Daily Mail* in response to the christening of Prince George in 2013.

I'm ... pleased that non-religious naming ceremonies are popular. For some people, it can be more honest to mark the joy of the formal welcome with a civil ceremony or a ritual of your own devising ... About one third of UK families fail to celebrate their new babies in any formal way, and I really do think they are missing out. Because whether it's a traditional baptism or a naming ceremony, an actual event acknowledges the importance of the new arrival in front of family and friends who bear witness.[9]

A search for *naming ceremony* in the national UK newspapers reveals that, prior to 1991, this idea is only ever mentioned connected with the dedication of new ships/trains/sports stadia, or referring to the practices of other countries/religions. In 1991, for the first time, a naming ceremony as a secular alternative to baptism is mentioned, offered by the Humanist Society.[10] We have seen that shortly after this, the Government intervened to offer naming ceremonies through local governments. In addition, Humanist and other options for naming ceremonies have gained in popularity.

In the twenty-first century, naming ceremonies have become established and normal, and are often paired together with *christenings* by companies offering services such as venues for parties or gifts (for example on Mothercare's website, which has a section for 'christening and naming day' gifts).[11] From about 2006 onwards, increasing references to celebrities holding naming ceremonies appeared in the British national newspapers,[12] and they featured in soap operas and other television programmes.[13]

People now have a wide variety of choice in types of ceremonies and celebrations to mark life events such as the birth of a child, often combining a naming ceremony with a first birthday or waiting and holding a ceremony for two or more children at once to mark the completion of a family. Naming ceremonies can be held to mark adoptions, or the formations of new family units formed through new relationships. They are also used by adults to mark changes in identity, especially gender transitions.[14]

This wide range of choices available is perhaps one advantage of naming ceremonies over baptism from the point of view of families. They are able to choose the venue, words for the ceremony, readings, music, symbolism, and who to conduct the ceremonies, most of which are inflexible for families seeking a christening in the Church of England. They are also able to choose any people to act as 'guideparents', rather than just those who have been christened, as for godparents at baptism. Indeed, they are even able to choose what to call these supporting adults, including the traditional title of *godparents*, which is still used by many at Humanist and other secular naming ceremonies.[15]

Consumerism in religion

This consumerist approach to rites of passage applies to baptism as well as to naming ceremonies. The increase that has been seen in the last few decades in the christening of older children has taken place for a variety of reasons. Families sometimes wait to have several children christened at once, or they may wait for the child's first birthday to combine both celebrations, or simply wait until they have the time, energy or money to organize an appropriate celebration. Additionally, there has probably also been a rise in churchgoing families choosing to have a service of Thanksgiving for new babies, allowing children to be baptized when they are old enough to make a decision for themselves. This was the choice my own parents made, allowing me to choose to be baptized at the age of seven.

This consumerist approach to religion is seen both within and outside of regular churchgoing communities. Gilliat-Ray's study of the prayer space in the Millennium Dome showed that those using it found the lack of any symbols of, and connection with, institutional religions was positively helpful in allowing them to construct their own spiritual experiences in the space in their own ways.[16] Many people now prefer to build their own sacred practices, using a variety of traditional and new images, practices and ideas to make a spiritual world that meets their own subjective needs and experiences.

This is not unique to New Age or alternative spiritualities, however. The Church has increasingly begun to address the needs of individuals, especially since the 1980s, when the 'entrepreneurial spirit'[17] of the Thatcher era extended to the Church. A greater variety of worship styles and specialized services and churches catered to the needs of particular groups in society. Liturgically, this increased choice and specialization of worship is seen in the development of the Common Worship liturgy, which expects clergy to build a service out of a range of liturgical options available, to suit the needs of the congregation and the occasion.

However, while this consumerist approach, common in secular society, has certainly had a strong impact on the Church, individualism always has limits in a church that regularly declares a common creed, gives precedence to the same Scriptures and inherited traditions, and shares a common liturgy. The beliefs and needs of individual members and the corporate body of the Church will inevitably be in tension at times, but to be a Christian means to travel within a community of faith, which may sometimes involve compromise.

Both the conservation and the discovery of truth must be primarily corporate endeavours. The twin dangers of excessive dogmatism and rootless individualism are to be guarded against not by rejecting all traditional restraints but by developing traditions which are able to stimulate and control individual exploration. Once this is understood, some at least of the stresses and strains which affect every living tradition can be seen to be inseparable from its continued growth.[18]

Do social uses have any place in religion?

This 'pick and mix' approach to rites of passage can make clergy and committed churchgoers feel very uncomfortable when applied to baptism. They do not want this essential sacrament to be used as one nice option among many to welcome a baby, but as a serious commitment to Christ and to the Church. Some clergy and churchgoers wish to sever the link between baptism and the human life cycle altogether, as argued by the Revd Tim Hayes in 2015 in the *Daily Express* newspaper.

Christenings and baptisms are nothing to do with the birth of a child. In our culture we assume when children are born we get them baptised. But it's not a naming ceremony, it's about expressing your whole-hearted commitment to Jesus Christ.[19]

While the ideas expressed by Hayes here are more forceful than most clergy would feel comfortable with, many clergy do feel very unhappy about the seemingly 'secular' uses of baptism discussed in this book. Church guidance to families seeking a christening tends to focus exclusively on the religious meanings of baptism and usually fails to mention the other meanings that the rite has for parents. Sometimes such guides speak of inappropriate uses of the rite. According to this perspective, baptism is primarily about becoming a Christian and joining the Church. Linking this with celebrating birth, naming a child, welcoming a child into the family or society, even making promises to the child other than to bring him or her up as a Christian, is a distraction from the rite's true meaning. This leaves clergy and regular churchgoers entirely at odds with non-churchgoing families seeking a christening about what is going on. For such families, the occasion is mainly about naming, welcoming, celebrating, promising love and commitment, and perhaps declaring an intention to bring the child up as a Christian or asserting membership of the Church. For regular churchgoers and clergy only the last of these is important, and it is often understood in a different way to that of non-churchgoing families. Some may regard all social uses as an abuse, whereas others may regard them as appropriate as secondary meanings, although in danger of becoming a distraction if the religious meanings are not taken seriously enough.

This labelling of some meanings, uses and aspects of the rite as 'religious' and others as 'social' is falling into the very common trap of assuming that these things can be separated. This is because the elements have become separated out in how churchgoers and clergy talk about baptism, as if it is possible to be concerned with beliefs and theology without also being concerned with relationships, stages of life and practices. This logocentric view of the world, in which words and ideas are focused on, to the exclusion of the visual, the physical, the practical, has in the past been the norm among theologians. Although some are challenging it now, it is all too easy to fall back into.

For many intellectuals and theologians, the word and the oral represent the most authoritative and reliable discourse. Mostly, the visual image is to be mistrusted as misleading, illusory and untrustworthy in its illusions and ambivalences. These 'logocentrics' are often strongly committed to substituting words for images, reducing figure to language, and generally subordinating the visual to the verbal.[20]

In Chapter 3 I argued that it was because they could not control the practical elements of baptism associated with the word *christening* in the Reformation era (family traditions, social significance, popular practices) that clergy disapproved of and downgraded these elements of the rite by avoiding using *christening*, in favour of the intellectual, theological, logocentric elements associated with *baptism*. In reality, however, religion is not just about beliefs, or about theology and ideas, but it is connected with every aspect of life.

> religion has everything to do with the relationships that constitute, form and enliven people in everyday activities in this material world ... Religion continues today when people eat or do not eat together, when they engage or do not engage in sexual activities, when they include or exclude strangers from their communities. To reach conclusions like these we need to reject the deeply ingrained notion that religion is belief in god.[21]

However orthodox a Protestant Christian, he or she does not in fact practise a religion that is only about a defined set of beliefs. Religion is always lived religion; it is always about practices as well as beliefs; it is always about relationships, both with other human beings and with sacred beings. So, it is certainly inevitable that there will always be social aspects to religious expressions, but should such social aspects be embraced or downplayed, as the Church has often done over the past 500 years (as reflected in their language use)? This depends on the view of the goodness of creation: does God work through humanity and sociality, or must these be transcended or bypassed for salvation to take place?

> A strong case can be made for this theological validation of the social construction of reality in terms of the doctrine of creation. The possibility that God may be revealed through social construction and socially constructed knowledge (culture and ideology), and not exclusively to inspired individuals, or to Church Councils, involves the idea that God created human persons essentially as social beings, whose sociality may be said to be a reflection of the sociality of the being of God as Trinity. The idea that divine revelation occurs within cultures, and not outside them, is a *sine qua non* of modern hermeneutic theory.[22]

A theology of baptism that does not touch the social realities of life, the human experience of a baby being born into a family and society, which does not touch the social bonds of that family, a theology that does not include the experiences of baptism found associated with the word *christening* in the discourse outside church life, can easily become a thin and disconnected theology. If religion does not touch real life, then it will have no real impact: it is just disconnected beliefs. The Church ignores these social uses of baptism, highlighted in this study, at its peril.

The view of this rite found commonly among non-churchgoers and associated with the word *christening* may sometimes be low in religious commitment, personal cost or doctrinal content. It does, however, celebrate social relationships, deep and self-giving love and relational commitment. These things, while not being enough to encapsulate the Christian faith or the importance of baptism inherited in the Christian tradition, are essential ingredients of a Christian lifestyle. Respect for parents and faithfulness in marriage are mentioned in the ten commandments (Exodus 20.12, 14), and Jesus spoke extensively on family and other social relationships (Mark 7.9–13), and placed the love of neighbour as the second of the two commandments that summarized all of the law (Matthew 22.37–40). The Book of Common Prayer marriage service describes marriage, the basis of family life, as

> an honourable estate, instituted of God in the time of man's innocency, signifying unto us the mystical union that is betwixt Christ and his Church; which holy estate Christ adorned and beautified with his presence, and first miracle that he wrought, in Cana of Galilee; and is commended of Saint Paul to be honourable among all men; and therefore is not by any to be enterprised, nor taken in hand, unadvisedly, lightly, or wantonly ... but reverently, discreetly, advisedly and soberly, and in the fear of God.[23]

Marriage is seen as a serious commitment of Christian life and the foundation of family life. The view of baptism found among non-churchgoers takes this commitment to family life very seriously indeed, even if those who hold it may not now see marriage as necessarily the foundation of this family life. The marriage-like vows that have developed outside of church circles as a meaning of christening come from solidly Christian roots and reflect the wisdom of Jesus and the teachings of the Church down the ages.

Conclusion

The making of marriage-like vows of love and commitment to children when they are christened is, therefore, a positive and thoroughly Christian and theologically defendable extension of the meaning of the rite. Churches would do much better to embrace and include this understanding of what it means, and use it as a point of connection with non-churchgoing families. This could then act as a starting point gently to introduce some of the meanings of the rite important to the churches. Clergy and church representatives have, in the past, seen their first job in preparing families for the baptism of their children as disillusioning them of the false understandings such as folk beliefs and social uses of the rite, before teaching them the 'true' meanings of the Church. This has not resulted in a better understanding of the rite, but rather in a disconnection and sometimes also an antipathy between such families and the Church. Such social uses of christening are not sufficient for a full understanding of the depths of meaning of the rite, but they are a good place to start from, to build trust, understanding and a relationship between the local church and families sympathetic to it who wish to have their children christened.

Notes

1 McKee, D. and McKee, H. (2011), 'The Christening Song with Lyrics', YouTube. Retrieved 24.1.17, from www.youtube.com/watch?v=ofrz077L2fg.

2 Hansard, HC Deb, 2 April 1990, vol. 170 cc914–85.

3 Bowlby, J. (2005), *A Secure Base: Clinical Applications of Attachment Theory*, London: Routledge, p. 1.

4 Hansard, HC Deb, 16 December 2003, vol. 415 cc212–34WH.

5 League of Nations (1924), *Geneva Declaration of the Rights of the Child*. Retrieved 6.2.17, from www.un-documents.net/gdrc1924.htm.

6 UN General Assembly (20 November 1959), *Declaration of the Rights of the Child*, A/RES/1386(XIV). Retrieved 3.2.17, from www.un.org/ga/search/view_doc. asp?symbol=A/RES/1386(XIV), principle 6, p. 20.

7 Hansard, HC Deb, 23 May 1995, vol. 260 cc732–3.

8 Hansard, HL Deb, 26 April 1995, vol. 563 cc911–3.

9 'Why in this Sceptical Age We Still All Love a Christening', *Daily Mail*, 25 October 2013.

10 *The Observer*, 12 May 1991, p. 71.

11 Mothercare (2016), 'Christening & Naming Day Gifts'. Retrieved 10.2.17, www.mothercare.com/gift/shop-by-occasion/christening-and-naming-day-gifts/.

12 For example, *The Sun*, 13 July 2016, p. 14.

13 For example, *Daily Mirror*, 8 April 2016, p. 33.

14 For example, *The Guardian*, 22 May 2015, and *Mail Online*, 24 July 2015.

15 British Humanist Association (2017), 'Humanist Namings FAQ'. Retrieved 27.1.17, from https://humanism.org.uk/ceremonies/humanist-namings/faqs/#7.

16 Gilliat-Ray, S. (2005), '"Sacralising" Sacred Space in Public Institutions: A Case Study of the Prayer Space at the Millennium Dome', *Journal of Contemporary Religion* 20(3), pp. 357–72.

17 Woodhead, L. and Catto, R. (eds) (2012), *Religion and Change in Modern Britain*, London: Routledge, p. 20.

18 The Doctrine Commission of the Church of England (1981), *Believing in the Church: The Corporate Nature of Faith*, London: SPCK, p. 23.

19 Tim Hayes, 'Unwed Parents' Fury over Baptism Snub', *Daily Express*, 29 May 2015.

20 Pattison, S. (2007), *Seeing Things: Deepening Relations with Visual Artefacts* London: SCM Press, p. 15.

21 Harvey, G. (2013), *Food, Sex and Strangers: Understanding Religion as Everyday Life*, Durham: Acumen, p. 2.

22 Northcott, M. (2000), 'Pastoral Theology and Sociology', in J. Woodward and S. Pattison (eds), *The Blackwell Reader in Pastoral and Practical Theology*, Oxford: Blackwell, p. 160.

23 Book of Common Prayer, pp. 301, 302.

6

Godparents

Sandra Millar argues that the giving of godparents is one of the most significant things for families seeking a christening, and yet is often neglected by churches. The research her team carried out into non-churchgoing parents' motivations to seek a baptism found that wanting their children to have godparents was the most common.

> Godparents are valued as people who will build a long-term stable relationship with the child, playing an active part in the child's life as a role model and offering nurture and guidance. Sometimes parents tend to project forwards into the teenage and young adult years, when a voice offering advice from outside the family might be appreciated.[1]

Millar points out that parents are often surprised by the lack of interest in godparents among the clergy they speak to. There is often no guidance offered about what it means to be a godparent, or how to choose a suitable person other than that they should be baptized. Godparents are not often invited to preparation sessions or rehearsals, and the giving of a certificate is often the only acknowledgement they receive from the church.

When I conduct a christening, I usually invite parents to choose a second, non-biblical, reading to help them feel involved in the planning of the occasion. In 2016 a family requested the following poem.

> Our precious little godchild
> We felt so truly blessed
> the day your parents asked us
> the day we answered 'yes'.
>
> We promise you through the years
> with all of life's demands
> our love for you will never change
> We're here with open hands.

A commitment of faith we bring to you
and our God above.
Forever and always and through life's years
you'll always have our love.[2]

Like the 'Christening Song' mentioned in the last chapter, which was also written by godparents to the children being christened, this poem expresses an attitude to baptism that sees the rite as being about promises to love and commitment to the flourishing of the child. Like the marriage-like vows between parents and children, the formation of a new relationship with godparents at a christening is a way in which the rite is used to form bonds between people in an attempt to provide a network of support for children and for their parents as they grow up.

From the Church's perspective, however, godparenthood is a very different thing. It is seen as being about teaching the child the Christian faith and offering spiritual guidance. This becomes another point on which the approaches of non-churchgoers and churchgoers diverge over the meaning of the rite. So how did this divergence emerge, and where does godparenthood come from?

Godparenthood in the history of the Church

From the second century onwards, two developments in the early Church led to the development of the tradition of sponsorship at baptism. The first was the increasing number of Gentile converts, making the informal practices of reception into the Church difficult and requiring someone to vouch for the sincerity of the convert and to help them through the baptismal process. The second was the increasing demand of Christian parents to have their children christened, which meant that someone was needed to make the promises on behalf of the child and to teach them about the faith as they grew up. Over the course of the first millennium, at different rates in different parts of the Christian world, sponsorship gained in importance in both the liturgy of baptism and in the instruction of children in the faith. The relationship between the baptized child and the sponsors increasingly became seen as one of spiritual parenthood, so that the sponsors became referred to as spiritual fathers and mothers, or in England godfathers and godmothers.[3] From the sixth to the ninth centuries, this pattern of spiritual kinship formed through sponsorship at a person's christening (by now usually of infant candidates) became a key feature of the kinship system in Western Europe. It was prized by many people as a way of forming kin relationships, in addition to through blood or marriage, and hence to forge alliances and turn strangers into kin:

> although blood kinsmen were one's most reliable friends and supporters, there was a disadvantage in that such kinship was contingent on the vagaries of biology and was inflexible when it came to integrating important or useful outsiders into the group. Various mechanisms to turn outsiders into kinsmen, including marriage alliances, were commonly used, but of all these spiritual kinship was the most popular. Spiritual kinsmen were especially prized because the bond created with them was a sacred one, rooted in God's grace. Furthermore, it was a bond of choice, made by mutual agreement.[4]

These spiritual kinship patterns were much more extensive than those known in the UK today between godparents and godchildren. They included forming a new bond between parents and their children's godparents (known as coparents). These bonds were taken very seriously, such that marriage between spiritual kin was prohibited, as for kin by marriage or blood. The Church valued spiritual kinship as a way of encouraging lay education in the faith, but, for the laity, the value was a mixture of economic, emotional, practical and spiritual. By the tenth century, the kinship created by sponsorship became reflected in the practice of godparents being allowed to give names to children when they were baptized, often giving them their own names as a sign of their spiritual bond.

The Reformers objected to the marriage prohibitions linked with spiritual kinship, but most retained godparenthood as a useful way of encouraging spiritual education in children after baptism. In the early seventeenth century, William Perkins argued that godparenthood should not be seen as forging spiritual kinship, but he did see sponsorship as forging a bond, symbolized in the name of the child. He said that godparents

> bind themselves by solemn promise, in the name of the child, before the whole church assembled, that they will be careful so soon as he comes to years of discretion that he be brought up in the fear and service of God, and be instructed in the principles of faith and repentance, and acquainted with the promise made by them in his behalf, that he may frame his life thereafter. (Perkins, 1606)[5]

The spiritual link between godparent and godchild remained important, although of a less kin-like nature, in the early years of the Protestant

Church in England. Naming after godparents was a common practice that persisted until the end of the sixteenth century. The practice formed a 'link between a person's name, his soul, and the protector of that soul – reflected in the transmission of the godparent's name'.[6]

The importance of godparents in a christening is seen in the tendency in the early years of Early Modern English (1500 to the early 1600s) to credit the godparents, rather than, or as well as, the priest/minister with instrumentality at the baptism. 'To christen' meant, among other things, 'to stand sponsor to [a child] at baptism',[7] which is given as an obsolete meaning in the *Oxford English Dictionary*. I very much found this to be the case in the texts that I studied. For example, Thomas Howard, at his trial for treason, described the relationship between Elizabeth I and her cousin Mary Queen of Scots. It seems that they became coparents through Queen Elizabeth's standing as godmother to Queen Mary's child (the future King James of Scotland and later of England), even though this was done in absentia:

> After this there grew Amity between the Queen's Majesty and the Scottish Queen; the Queen took her for her Friend, sent Ambassador unto her, and **christened** (**christned**) her Child; all this excluded Enmity. (Thomas Howard, 1571, trial of Thomas Howard)[8]

Similarly, this quotation from the early seventeenth century shows how both godparents and priest (or in this case archbishop) were equally seen as agents in the baptizing of a child:

> Casaubon had a son lately borne here, and **christened** (**christned**) by the King and the Lord of Canterbury, whose deputies for the purpose were the bishops of Bath and Welles, and Rochester. (Letter from John Chamberlain to Ralph Winwood, 1612)[9]

Over the course of the seventeenth century, however, this use of the term *christened* declined and fell into disuse. Godparents no longer routinely gave their names to their godchildren. It seems that the distrust of godparenthood among the Reformers, and especially of the fictional kinship system that was forged through baptism, succeeded in eroding the importance of godparenthood in early Protestant England. However, despite this, sponsorship continued to play a significant role in social life. It is seen in the eighteenth century, for example, as being important in establishing identity for people of African descent, as full citizens and human beings, as Christians who are integrated with the native population. At the Old Bailey trial of John Wright in 1736 for theft from a man of African descent, the following fascinating exchange between these two people shows how important godparenthood was to people like Thomas Farrow, allowing him to become an insider and his words to be trusted, thus extending the protection of the courts to him. John Wright was found guilty and sentenced to transportation.

> Farrow, (a Negro) [*sic*]. I was going down Queen-street and this Man, (pointing to the Prisoner) took my Hat from my Head ... I cried stop Thief, and followed him close at his Heels to an Alley that goes into Bow-Lane ...
>
> Prisoner. Ask him if he has been **baptized** (**baptiz'd**)?
>
> Farrow. Yes, my Lord Grantham was my Godfather. (1736, Trial of John Wright for theft)[10]

Smith-Bannister points to the practice of using sponsorship at baptism as a means of providing for the needs of illegitimate and abandoned children in the late sixteenth and early seventeenth centuries. The person standing godparent for such a child would give him or her their first name, and in the case of foundlings their surname would usually be the name of the street on which they were found. The godparent would also promise to take responsibility for the child, saving the parish the costs of raising them. 'In a time of short life expectancy and high illegitimacy ... godparents were a second set of parents providing a safety net for children without natural parents to support them.'[11]

Over the course of the seventeenth century the practice of naming after godparents declined and naming after parents increased. In addition, paternal kin were increasingly used as sponsors at baptism, making the family increase in importance and godparenthood decline. Does this represent what Lynch describes as the 'withering'[12] of the practice of spiritual kinship in northern Europe as a result of the Reformation? Certainly, it lost much of its status as a significant social factor in society. However, there is still great importance attached to godparenthood by many in English society today.

Godparenthood today

While the practice of spiritual kinship has lost its implications of forming new kin relationships, resulting in marriage prohibitions as if they were blood or marriage kin, the practice of using christening as a means of giving godparents to children is still very much alive and important in some families. This may not form new kin, but it does cement friendship relationships into officially recognized relationships that bond together not only godparent and godchild but also whole families. Graham Allan argues that one of the key differences between kinship and friendship relationships in modern Britain is that friendships are generally much more subject to change than kinship relationships; the vast majority of friendships 'wax and wane',[13] and only a very few will last a lifetime. While, as with marriages, not all relationships forged through sponsorship will last a lifetime, by choosing godparents for their child, parents are declaring an intention that the relationship will last, thus making this friendship officially recognized and durable in a way that has some of the features of kinship. A key feature of kinship that the godparent–godchild relationship shares is that it is asymmetrical, not expecting favours to be returned, whereas friendships are usually expected to be symmetrical. Many people still believe that one of the key roles of a godparent is to look after the child should their parents die, and there is some confusion about whether this tradition has legal status or not (which it doesn't). This belief is reflected in the role of Sirius Black in the Harry Potter books, who, as Harry's godfather, is seen as able to sign parental forms for him and invites the orphaned Harry to come to live with him. Interestingly, godparenthood is a major theme in several of the books, as the orphaned Potter hopes to be rescued from his terrible aunt and uncle by the discovery of a previously unknown godfather. However, while godparenthood is mentioned frequently, baptism or christening is entirely absent from the books; godparenthood has taken on a life and significance beyond the ritual from which it came.[14]

The Life Events team's website, the Church Support Hub, has a large section that explains to clergy and church members the importance of godparents to families:

> The choice of godparents often honours long friendships, and in choosing them, parents are envisaging a relationship that will last at least 20 years, probably a lifetime. In the research, the biggest reason (by a small margin) that parents gave for wanting their child to be christened was to ensure he or she had godparents. So it is almost impossible to overstate the importance of godparents to families and this needs acknowledging and applauding. Parents also come wanting their child to have the best start in life and God's blessing on them. This can lead into conversations about how parents and godparents can 'be a blessing' in their child's life.[15]

The fact that the Church Support Hub website needed to state this so strongly reflects the fact that, for many churches, godparents are not considered very important. In my own training in ministry, I was not encouraged to meet godparents before the day of the christening, nor to talk to parents about their choices, other than to check that prospective godparents were baptized. I would not usually remember the names of the godparents and was not taught to name them in the prayers. Other than standing up and making the promises during the service, there is little left for godparents to do in the christening.

This lack represents a decline of strong emphasis on the importance of godparents for churches since the early years of the Church of England. In the Book of Common Prayer, godparents were the ones who made the promises on behalf of the child. It is they, and not the parents, to whom the priest addressed the statement, 'Ye have brought *this* Child here to be baptized',[16] and it is to the godparents that he addressed the demand 'Name this Child'.[17] In the catechism, children were taught to believe that it was their godparents who brought them to be christened, and to credit them for all the spiritual benefits this involved.[18] With this important role for godparents it is easy to see why, in Early Modern English, they were regarded as instrumental to the baptism, such that they were the ones to *christen* the child. The idea that it is the godparents who are responsible for the baptism of the child would seem impossible in the modern Church of England. The godparents have become minor players in the service, standing beside and supporting the parents in the commitments they make to bring up the child as a Christian. In the revision of the liturgy for the Alternative Service Book, all the instructions and exhortations are addressed to the 'parents and godparents' together.[19] They have no role of their own, other than to say 'Amen' after the baptism. In the Common Worship service, there is no role at all for godparents that is not shared with parents. This reflects the reality of how children are brought up and the importance of parents in the spiritual development of children. However, in the removal of the traditional liturgical roles for godparents, Common Worship has little significance left for the godparents. Godparenthood has become a vestigial feature of the baptism service, kept because of tradition but with no real content. This decline in the importance of godparents in the Church has roots in the thought of the Reformers, for whom godparenthood was kept for reasons of expediency, another layer of protection to ensure that children are taught the faith, but with no unique responsibilities.

> Calvin and the Reformed tradition ... retained sponsorship, but in a very attenuated form. They shared Luther's contempt for the marital impediments rooted in baptismal sponsorship and rejected entirely the notion of spiritual kinship as an impediment to marriage .... [they]

placed natural parents on a par with sponsors for the future religious formation of the child; they even countenanced parents sponsoring their own children ... Thus the sponsor's role was emptied of content as the stress was placed on the parents' responsibility for their own children.[20]

Advice from churches about bringing a child to baptism often expresses the difficulty that this puts the church in, with regard to godparents. Books aimed at explaining what baptism means to parents show signs of tension about godparenthood and concerns that families are not really taking it seriously:

> there is often a real tension between being as welcoming as we can to the enquiry, while trying to encourage a choice of godparents who recognize that the role is not merely honorary or social, and who are ready for a long-term, serious and spiritual undertaking.[21]

In the booklet *Your Baby's Baptism in the Anglican Church*, there is one small section about godparents on the side of one of 14 pages of advice. The assumptions that many in the Church hold about the lack of seriousness with which families seeking a christening have in their choice of godparents is seen in the advice that 'Godparents are chosen to help your child become more godly – not just to give good presents!'[22]

However, the assumption behind this, that parents do not take godparenthood seriously but the Church does, is the reverse of what many parents experience when they approach a church for a christening. The Church maintains the tradition of godparents because it is required by its foundations, because they are so important in the Book of Common Prayer, and possibly partly also because it is widely expected by parents. Priests speak to parents about the importance of godparents being baptized, and emphasize the commitment to teach children about the faith, but they often do not really expect godparents to take this commitment seriously. This attitude on the part of the Church can clash terribly with many parents' understanding of baptism and the importance they attach to godparents. This is seen in a discussion on the online chat forum Mumsnet in 2013, which reflects the conflicts many parents feel between their needs and the attitudes of Church:

> I got the paperwork to fill in today and 'godparents' have to be christened with at least one being confirmed. Even though I'm not sure what I believe, choosing godparents is still important to me as people who will be there for our children should anything happen to us ... I don't want to have to choose other people just because they are christened. I want

to choose the very best people for my child in the future … So AIBU [am I being unreasonable] to just tick 'christened' even though they aren't? And what are the chances of being caught out?[23]

While the mother who posted this question may seem to be an example of parents not taking the christening seriously – just as many regular churchgoers and clergy fear – her comments do reveal something about the importance of godparents. For her, the demands of the Church to choose only people who have been christened is not giving the message to take godparents seriously, but that she should compromise and choose people who would be less committed to the role and less likely to stay in touch. She feels she is asked just to tick a box, to say that they are baptized, which seems irrelevant to her. The responses on the chat thread to this question show that she had mixed responses to her dilemma. Some saw godparents as being all about 'religious guidance' (as in the first two responses below) and others as being about the support they give the child in all areas of life (the third quotation below):

> Godparents are not there should anything happen to you, they are there to ensure that your your dc [darling child] receives a religious upbringing. Are your potential godparents regular church-goers, even if not christened themselves?

> YABU [you are being unreasonable]. If you don't really want your child christened, and you want to pick 'special people' who are not themselves Christians, then it seems rather silly to have a christening.

> Tick the box. If you know that they're the right choice for your child then that's all that matters, IMHO [in my humble opinion]. Why should the fact that they haven't been christened themselves make them somehow 'unsuitable'?

Godparenthood has taken on a whole world of meaning of its own, which the Church has lost contact with and been left behind from. Our mistrust of the motivations of ordinary families seeking christenings has led us to lose our own vision for what this role means, and we are in danger of simply becoming 'a church that likes to say "no"'.[24]

The Church needs to emphasize and reclaim the importance of godparents praying for their godchildren and sharing the faith with them. However, this should not be at the cost of discarding the vision that families have for godparents. Christianity is a religion of relationship; it worships a trinitarian God and calls all our fellow Christians 'brother' and 'sister' (Mark 3.35). Forming a kinship that goes beyond families is a thoroughly Christian idea. The Church would do better to affirm and build on this foundation than ignore and dismiss it, as it has too often done.

Godparenthood and evangelization

Christianity in Western Europe has seen a collapse of the ability of Christian families to pass their faith on to their children. This is not so much due to a failure of churches as to a failure of family life to nurture children in their Christian faith. For the vast majority of people, this is how faith is kindled and grown, and in so many cases in modern Britain this is where faith has not been passed down. The work of the Church, if it is to be effective in evangelization, is more about supporting and encouraging families to be places where faith is nurtured than about telling people directly about the good news of Jesus (although this will be important too). It will do this more effectively if we build on the social networks that already exist, and help give people tools to live out faith in everyday family life. Godparenthood already has great, perhaps even growing, meaning in today's world. The Church would do well to include godparents in the preparation of families for a christening, perhaps give them resources of prayers they can use for their godchildren, or children's Bible stories to read to them. Perhaps we could keep in touch over the years, with godparents as well as parents, inviting them with their godchildren to Messy Church, toddler services, Godparent Sunday services, and other family-friendly events that teach the faith in a fun and accessible way. Certainly, we should be proud and not embarrassed about the inheritance of the institution of godparenthood, and should aim to affirm and recognize the importance of this vital aspect of modern baptism.

Notes

1 Millar, S. (2018), *Life Events: Mission and Ministry at Baptisms, Weddings and Funerals*, London: Church House Publishing, p. 41.

2 www.abernook.com (2005), 'To My Godchild', Pinterest. Retrieved 8.2.17, from https://uk.pinterest.com/pin/192388215306457266/.

3 Lynch, J. (1986), *Godparents and Kinship in Early Medieval Europe*, Princeton: Princeton University Press, p. 5.

4 Lynch (1986), *Godparents*, p. 337.

5 *The whole treatise of the cases of conscience*, Early English Books Online.

6 Smith-Bannister, S. (1997), *Names and Naming Patterns in England, 1538–1700*, Oxford: Clarendon Press, p. 27.

7 *OED* Online (2016).

8 Corpus of English Dialogues, D1TNORFO.

9 Parsed Corpus of Early English Correspondence, Chamber, 26.

10 Old Bailey Proceedings, t17360115-31

11 Smith-Bannister (1997), *Names and Naming*, pp. 31, 32.

12 Lynch (1986), *Godparents*, p. 57.

13 Allan, G. (1996), *Kinship and Friendship in Modern Britain*, Oxford: Oxford University Press, p. 94.

14 Rowling, J. K. (1999), *Harry Potter and the Prisoner of Azkaban*, London: Bloomsbury.

15 Archbishops' Council (2015), 'The Importance of Godparents', Church Support Hub. Retrieved 24.1.17, from https://churchsupporthub.org/baptisms/explore-thinking/importance-godparents/.

16 Book of Common Prayer, p. 266.

17 Book of Common Prayer, p. 269.

18 Book of Common Prayer, p. 289.

19 Church of England (1980), *The Alternative Service Book 1980, together with the Liturgical Psalter*, London: Hodder & Stoughton, p. 245.

20 Lynch (1986), *Godparents*, p. 23. Parentheses added.

21 Earey, M., Lloyd, T. and Tarrant, I. (2007), *Connecting with Baptism: A Practical Guide to Christian Initiation Today*, London: Church House Publishing, p. 70.

22 Thomas, S. (2000), *Your Baby's Baptism in the Anglican Church*, Stowmarket: Kevin Mayhew, p. 9.

23 Mumsnet (2013), 'To Lie to the Church about Our Godparents?' Retrieved 18.1.17, from www.mumsnet.com/Talk/am_i_being_unreasonable/1747281-To-lie-to-the-church-about-our-godparents. Parentheses added.

24 Woodhead, L. (2016), 'Why "No Religion" is the New Religion'. Retrieved 24.5.17, from www.youtube.com/watch?v=hPLsuW-TCtA.

7

'Just an excuse for a party':
Joy and celebration in baptism

It is one of the most common complaints heard against families seeking a christening within the Church that 'it's just an excuse for a party'. Interestingly enough, this suspicion of the motives of non-churchgoing parents who bring their children for baptism is often shared by those who are actively and self-consciously secular. The chat thread on the popular parents' website Mumsnet in 2013, mentioned in the last chapter, reflected these tensions very well:

> Christening your child isn't a nice party, it's welcoming your child into the church. Godparents are meant to provide religious guidance, not just to 'be there for your child'.
>   I'm not at all religious (and therefore haven't had my children christened), but I'm still quite [thinking emoji] at the idea of lying to a church. If you're not faithful enough that lying to the minister and congregation bothers you then why are you having your child christened into the church at all?[1]

Behind the argument that a christening should not be just 'a nice party' are two assumptions: one is that having a party is frivolous and insubstantial, and the other is that wanting a party is the real reason behind the event. This book has explored many of the reasons that ordinary people give for having a christening. The reasons and motivations vary from family to family, but common themes are: the giving and public acknowledgement of a name; recognizing the child as an individual and member of the family and of society, before God and others; the making of marriage-like vows of love and commitment to the child; the introduction of the child into the family and into society; and the giving of godparents. These motivations are not simply religious, neither are they purely secular. They have strands of both running through them, woven together into the fabric of life, in which social realities and human relationships exist in a complex web of traditions, beliefs (even if these are rather vague and unarticulated) and values. God is not at the centre of this vision of what it means to christen a child, but God is also not absent and irrelevant. The party is a public celebration and acknowledgement of what really matters in having a child baptized, which is this complex web of difficult-to-articulate meanings and motivations.

So, the argument that the party is the real reason seems very unlikely. If they wanted a party they could much more easily arrange one without the discomfort of coming into the unfamiliar and threatening setting of a church, speaking to the forbidding and frightening vicar, braving the snide comments of the congregation members who resent their presence in 'our church', and jumping through whatever hoops of preparation the church chooses to set for baptism families.

The other problem with the allegation that baptism is 'just an excuse for a party' for some families is that, in Christian tradition, parties are far from frivolous and insubstantial. There is strong biblical precedent for parties being important and significant. Jesus was well known for his scandalous tendency to attend parties (John 2.1–11; Matthew 9.9–13; 11.16–19). He compared the kingdom of God to a wedding feast (Matthew 22.2) and used an extravagant party as the culmination of the story of the prodigal son (Luke 15.22–24). The Old Testament law contained many commands to the people of Israel to have particular feasts and celebrations, such as the Passover (Exodus 12.14), the Festival of Weeks (Exodus 34.22) and the Festival of Booths (Leviticus 23.40–43), and it also records celebrations for particular events like the bringing of the ark to Jerusalem (1 Chronicles 15.27–29) and the dedication of the Temple (2 Chronicles 7.8–10). Heaven is pictured as a place that erupts with joyful celebration over the repentance of a sinner (Luke 15.10) and of perpetual rejoicing (Revelation 12.12). Parties and celebration are not just social froth; they are commanded by God as integral parts of the faith. To fail to celebrate something does not mean that it is being taken more seriously, but that it is not being given its due significance.

Semantic prosody revisited

In chapter 2, I argued that *baptism* and *christening* have different 'feels', known as semantic prosody, due to the words with which they are frequently found in company. *Baptism*'s semantic prosody is much more sober and serious than that of *christening*. *Baptism* is associated with suffering in the figures of speech based on these words ('baptism of fire', 'it was a tough baptism'). Figures of speech featuring *christening*, on the other hand, are associated much more with celebration ('let's christen the new champagne flutes').

Collocates of these words (that is, words found frequently nearby to them) reflect this 'feel' or semantic prosody. *Baptism*'s collocates are much more sober and serious, often linked with death and sadness, like *funeral* and *death*. They are also more associated with overt religious commitments and language, often being linked with words like *God*, *Christian*, *communion* and *confirmation*. This reflects the seriousness with which clergy and churchgoers regard baptism. While it is an occasion for joy and celebration, this would not be over-emphasized because of the seriousness of the promises made, to follow Jesus, to believe in the Christian faith, to reject sin and evil and to turn to Christ.

The association between baptism and suffering and death has roots in the New Testament, for example in Paul's teaching that baptism is into Jesus' death (Romans 6.4). There is a sense that, while baptism is a joyful occasion of new birth, this is only a birth that comes about if candidates are first willing to die to sin and to give up their old life (John 12.24; Matthew 16.24–26). It is also seen in the Gospels' accounts of Jesus' teachings, in which *baptism* is a metaphor for death and suffering (Mark 10.38).

Conversely, *christening* seems to be the word that most encapsulates the celebratory side of this rite for British English speakers. The word can equally well refer to either the service in church or to the celebration afterwards in the pub or at home; *christening* is the entire event, whereas *baptism* is simply the part that occurs at the font. In this sense, the Church of England's assertion that the most helpful way of putting it is that 'during the christening your child will be baptized' is useful because it brings these two sides of the ritual together in a sentence that is meaningful to families.

So, should we regard this rite as a serious *baptism* or as a celebratory *christening*? I would argue, from a theological point of view, it must be both, as either is impoverished and diminished without the other. The rite of Christian initiation is a serious and life-changing commitment; in it we are reborn and this is a cause of great celebration. If, as a Church, we exclude the word *christening* (which is what the Church in England has mostly done for the last 500 years), then we cut off from our understanding of the rite an essential humanity. We potentially become the po-faced, kill-joys who cannot understand joy and celebration. This is not religious but rather irreligious, proudly promoting our own self-importance and denying our own creatureliness before God.

the Christian doctrine of creation implies that we are fundamentally non-serious, yet meaningfully loved. The very fabric of our lives – the creatureliness of our existence, we might say – is delightful, the end of graceful love, which suggests that our attempts to defend or justify what we are somehow miss the truth of our existence. This is perhaps why a saint such as Francis of Assisi remains so influential within the Church. His wandering life of radical simplicity – his tireless work to rebuild Christ's Church – was underwritten by his sense of being a fool for God ... we are unnecessary creatures in whom God freely delights. When we take ourselves too seriously, we thereby fall into sin. We need to be light-hearted for God.[2]

Pastoral implications of celebrations and parties

I would be very pleased if I never again heard the complaint 'they only want a christening as an excuse for a party'. Our churches need to become places of welcome and positive affirmation, not places where people are written off and their motivations questioned and judged. Instead of being suspicious of families, we need to become churches that celebrate along-side them. We need to be people who rejoice with those who are rejoicing and weep with those who are weeping (Romans 12.15). In joining in with their celebrations to welcome and rejoice at the life of a child, we can begin to open up the wonderful cause for celebration found in the love of God and the salvation God extends as a gift towards humankind. If we begin where people are, in the love and wonder of human life, and if we can build a real relationship through the process of christening the children of a family, then we can over time start to open up the true depths of love found in the God of love. This may only be begun in the christen-ing service itself. It will need ongoing relationship to build on it, through repeated invitations to Christmas, mothers' day, godparents' Sunday, Harvest, Messy Church, or whatever your church offers for families. But over time, if the relationship is maintained, then the story of the faith can begin to be shared. Once this pearl of great price (Matthew 13.45–46) is within sight, then the idea that this rite has deep and serious themes and demands for sacrifice may become a cost that is meaningful and joyful, rather than boring and difficult. *Baptism* and *christening* encapsulate the two aspects of the love of God and the love within families that this rite demands of us: it is a love that is both self-giving and sacrificial as well as celebratory and joyful. The former of these will not come across as meaningful or desirable unless framed within the context of the latter; it is in the love of God that service becomes perfect freedom.

Notes

1 Mumsnet (2013), 'To Lie to the Church about Our Godparents?' Retrieved 18.1.17, from www.mumsnet.com/Talk/am_i_being_unreasonable/1747281-To-lie-to-the-church-about-our-godparents.

2 Harvey, L. (2012), 'How Serious is it Really? The Mixed Economy and the Light-hearted Long Haul', in G. Cray and I. Mobsby (eds), *Fresh Expressions of Church and the Kingdom of God*, Norwich: Canterbury Press, pp. 101, 104.

8

Yes, but is it really *Christian* baptism?

I have argued that for families who do not regularly go to church, and yet seek to have their children christened, a baptism has a wealth of meanings and importance, of which the Church is frequently unaware. I have argued that there is theological validity in many of these meanings, and that the Church would benefit from remembering the importance of giving names, marking the introduction of a child into society, making vows of love and commitment to children, and the giving of godparents, as well as an appropriate celebration, with a good party. These things are important and have a spiritual as well as social significance. But are they enough together to give a full picture of a Christian doctrine of baptism? From my perspective as an Anglican priest, no, I don't think they do. There is more to 'christen-ing', becoming a Christian, than these things, although without them it is hard to see how a family can be truly Christian. There is more to the Christian faith than the recognition of individuals, families and societies; yet we may have good cause to doubt the authenticity of the faith of someone who does not show love and commitment to people, families and societies and a desire for their well-being. In the Christian faith we live out our lives as embodied people, with names that give us recognition as individuals known by God and by others, in relationship with our families, communities and nations. We do this as people who have submitted to the loving rule of one God, Father, Son and Holy Spirit. We are a community of people who tell the stories of this God: how God has created the world, including human-kind; how God has sought us and saved us, and met us in God's Son, Jesus of Nazareth.

However, there are two problems with the statement that the mean-ings of *christening* identified here are important but not sufficient to constitute Christian baptism. One is the assumption, easily made, that for non-churchgoing families who request a baptism these social mean-ings are the *only* meanings that they perceive, and that they have no genuinely religious motivation. The second problem with this statement is the question, 'Whose rite is it anyway?' Why should I have the right to define baptism, and those baptized Christians who do not come to church cannot? I will come on to address this second problem in the next chapter. In this chapter we will examine the first, and ask whether Christian baptism is really what families want, or if we would do better to point many of them in the direction of some alternative service to mark the birth of their children.

'All they want is a naming ceremony'

Baptism without *christening* becomes stale and cold, a harsh creed that commands doctrinal correctness but forgets human love. *Christening* without *baptism* becomes shallow and detached from the source of its meaning and significance. It is no wonder that the number of families seeking a christening for their children has dropped so dramatically in recent decades, if a christening is about no more than giving a name and promising love, and recognizing a person as part of a family and community. These are important things, but they are adequately provided for by holding a secular naming ceremony. For some parents, as they drift further from their families' historic connections with the Church, a naming ceremony will feel much more appropriate. Many of the people on Mumsnet (in the chat thread discussed in the last couple of chapters) who responded to the mum who wondered whether or not to lie about their proposed godparents' baptismal status, urged her to have such a ceremony:

> It doesn't sound like you want a christening, it sounds like you want a naming ceremony and a nice day out.

> YABU [you are being unreasonable]. Not a great way to set out on a Christian upbringing by lying at the Baptism. Why are you getting your child baptised if you don't go to church or believe in God? You can have people being important in your DC's [darling child's] life without a baptism.

> I also think a non-religious naming ceremony would be the way to go – or even a compromise of a naming ceremony with a religious blessing? If you're not really interested in the churchy/religious bit but want the family celebration and choosing godparents, then just do the bits you want![1]

For many people, to have a naming ceremony is entirely the right decision. It feels right to reach out to the Church at these key moments, as the mum who asked the original question in this chat thread did, and for families like this there may be a lot of missional mileage in the Church offering naming ceremonies. The Church has many years of experience in guiding families through ceremonies like this to mark key life events, and many people still feel a sense of connection with their local church and may appreciate this renewal of the link. From the Church's point of view, it is entirely within our mission to build the kingdom of God through the offering of services such as this, which strengthen families and encourage commitment in loving relationships. And there is the added bonus that offering naming ceremonies could help us to build up meaningful relationships with the people in our parishes and areas, to share the good news and to help others to see that the Church is a living and attractive community of faith. This will take work, and will need appropriate follow up, just like baptism does.

But so often, when parents are offered an alternative to baptism, such as a service of Thanksgiving, they are not impressed. This is not what they want, they want a proper christening, with the water. And naming ceremonies, while they have become normal and recognized, have so far failed to take over the ritual needs of most families who no longer choose baptism. Most families have not moved from christening their children to holding a naming ceremony; they have simply ceased having any ceremony to welcome new babies. They may take part in more low-key practices that have elements of ritual about them, like a baby shower, but a public and formal ceremony to mark a birth is now much less common than it once was. There seems to be a loss in this: ritual is an essential feature of how we make sense of the world and share common values, stories and ideas. The decline in baptism perhaps does not just represent a decline in people making a commitment to Christian faith for their children, but also a decline in public ceremonial to mark the birth of a new member of the family and society. This is a cause for concern for us as Christians, if we are committed to the flourishing of individuals and of society. Thanksgiving services do not really have any credence with most people in society at large, but people do understand a naming ceremony. As a Christian I would like to see more of these, both conducted by the Church and in secular settings, because I think it is good for children, families and society.

But there is a paradox in the changing patterns of ceremonial to mark life events. While a smaller proportion of families have any ceremony, when they do have one it tends to be a much bigger event than baptisms were in previous centuries. There are more guests, the events often take longer to plan and are more elaborate, and indeed the churches usually put much more time and preparation into baptism families than was common prior to the mid-twentieth century.

Why are so many (albeit a decreasing number of) non-churchgoing families seeking to go through the discomfort of approaching an unfamiliar institution to request a religious rite rather than having a secular naming ceremony? The research that was commissioned by the Life Events team into the attitudes of non-regular churchgoers who had had children baptized found that among the complex mixture of motivations there was often a sense of wanting the child to belong to the Church and to start their journey as a Christian,[2] although what they meant by these things will certainly be different from what most clergy think they mean.

Of course, the motivation will vary from family to family. For some, there may be pressure from parents or grandparents, but I think that this expectation is declining fast in the vast majority of places in the UK, though perhaps still present in pockets for some families in more traditional or rural communities. But the social expectation has largely disappeared; for most people, when they have their children baptized, this is a positive choice and a deliberate decision to do something different from many of their peers.

It is apparent that many non-regular churchgoers do not see any contradiction in saying that they want to bring their children up as Christians without regularly bringing them to church. To them, being a Christian does not necessarily entail regular churchgoing. They have, in other words, a very different concept of what baptism means, what kind of commitment it demands, what it means to be a Christian or a part of the Church, compared with regular churchgoers.

Church and sect ecclesiologies and their impact on baptism

The mother who asked on Mumsnet if she should lie to the church about the fact that her chosen godparents were not christened asked, 'Am I being unreasonable?' Several of the respondents clearly thought she wasn't being unreasonable at all. They understood that, for her, the choice of godparents was about who would be present in her child's life, not who would teach the child about the Christian faith. They were more likely to see the Church as being unreasonable to ask that godparents should be baptized, when it seemed completely unrelated to a godparent's task:

> Tick the box. If you know that they're the right choice for your child then that's all that matters, IMHO [in my humble opinion]. Why should the fact that they haven't been christened themselves make them somehow 'unsuitable'?

IMHO [in my humble opinion] the church are foolish to ask as it only encourages dishonesty, and why can't anyone be a godparent that the parents choose? However we didn't have ours christened but had other types of welcoming parties for them which were just as fun![3]

However, others, as seen in the replies quoted at the start of this chapter, saw it as entirely inappropriate, and argued that godparents should be about teaching the children the Christian faith, and therefore should be baptized. They stated, 'You are being unreasonable.' This question of what is or is not reasonable is based on an assumed shared set of values, an understanding of what reasonableness means. In this case, different people within society are operating with a different set of assumptions, and therefore what seems reasonable to one seems completely unreasonable to others. To committed and churchgoing Christians, and also to many secular people who have cut any historic ties their families may have once had to the Church, it is assumed that churchgoing is an essential part of the commitment that parents are taking on when they have their children christened. The Church they are imagining and talking about is a sectarian church, a gathering of highly committed individuals, who have all made a specific act of commitment to the beliefs and moral standards of the Church. Much is expected of individual members, and they are likely to see themselves as clearly distinct from the surrounding society. Sectarian-type churches, or congregational churches as Linda Woodhead calls them, have historically tended not to have infant baptism, since membership of the Church is an active choice by those old enough to make such a serious commitment. The Church of England has not been, for most of its history, a sectarian church, but a church-type or societal church. Societal churches usually begin from the assumption that all members of society are members, unless they specifically reject it or are from a group of outsiders. A 'church-type' church is institutional, hierarchical, closely allied to secular authorities, sacramental and includes all people. Membership of this type of church, according to Max Weber, is by birth and baptism.[4] This is why Cranmer insisted that all babies should be christened as soon after birth as possible. Catechesis, understanding of the faith and taking part in religious practices, would be taught by a Christian society as the child grew up, but the starting point was that all belonged, and all were expected to conform to Anglican belief and practice (even if, in reality, 'all' never did).

As with all models, each church is neither entirely one nor the other. The Church of England, as the established Church in England but also as expressed in congregations that are sometimes more and sometimes less open to their communities, is no exception to this. There are elements of both types of church in the Church of England, sometimes more one and sometimes more the other, but overall the Church seems to be moving in an increasingly congregational direction. This movement has created tensions with the societal foundations of the Church, and with the society that the Church has spent 500 years teaching that all belong to and all should and can be christened as members of it.

This is not the first time the Christian Church has changed over time such that its rituals become ill fitting to the needs of the day. In fact, this seems to have happened in the opposite direction in the first millennium AD. In the early years of the Church's history, it was very much a sectarian church, being an often-persecuted minority that rejected mainstream Roman religion and society. In the first centuries of the life of the Church, baptism was a serious affair for which candidates were often rigorously prepared, and membership of the Church demanded great commitment and special knowledge. When Christendom arose, this sectarian model became inappropriate, as whole societies became Christian and the Church was closely allied to the State. The Church became a societal church, and by the late first millennium almost all babies were baptized soon after birth in Christian Europe. Nevertheless, the rite of baptism was remarkably unchanged. David Wright argues that, even after nearly a millennium of universal infant baptism, 'infants were still being baptized by an awkward adaptation of a rite formulated for the baptism of responding believers'.[5]

> Baptism migrated from being an initiation rite to being a birth rite. This shift created a problem, since it left a gap in the Christian ritual system. Originally, baptism was, among other things, a ceremonial guarantee of participation in communion, but Holy Communion assumed a kind of knowledge that no infant could possibly possess.[6]

The question of whether christening should be seen as a birth rite or return to its original use as a rite of initiation and proclamation of commitment was, like many other aspects of Christian life, re-examined during the Reformation. But the Anabaptists, who advocated restricting baptism only to believers, changing the Church into a confessional body (thus making the Church more sectarian), lost the argument in the mainstream Reformation to Luther and Calvin, who advocated paedobaptism. The Reformers were keen to keep a church of the masses, fearing that the Church would lose its power and influence to enforce a Christian society if only those who were of strong religious convictions were baptized.

The Church of England was founded upon the assumption that the whole nation must have a common religion, under the headship of the monarch, and any deviance from this was treasonable, since it was in a common religion that the nation was held together under the headship of the monarch. But these medieval assumptions grew less tenable over time, especially in the eighteenth century, due to the Enlightenment and the disturbing ideas coming out of the French Revolution. Religion was gradually privatized, and no longer provided the unifying focus for society that it had in the post-Reformation era. In the nineteenth century, both within and outside the Church, questions were beginning to be asked about the desirability of having such a close connection between Church and State. This led to the emancipation of Roman Catholics and Nonconformists, and to the beginnings of questions being asked within the Church of England about the validity of the practice of baptizing all English people, as seen in the Gorham case in 1847.

In the nineteenth century, there was an effort by many clergy to make baptism a more solemn occasion. The large numbers of candidates made these ceremonies often rather riotous, and little effort was generally made to prepare families for the christening. This description of a baptism in the mid-nineteenth century was far from unusual:

> The ceremony of **baptising** then begins; one minister takes the boys and another the girls; but before the conclusion of the words that are repeated to all, there exists a scene of confusion and noise not consistent with so solemn an ordinance; the children crying and the mothers in vain endeavouring to appease them; some talking, others walking, notwithstanding the efforts of the four apparitors. (1855, The Marquess of Blandford, House of Commons)[7]

There was increasing concern among clergy and committed churchgoers in the nineteenth and early twentieth centuries about the association between baptism and 'folk religion'. When the 1836 Act of Registration came into effect, many clergy felt that requests for baptism would drop dramatically as it was believed that it meant nothing more to people than to give a name and register a birth. Well into the nineteenth century, Walter Hook wrote: 'Nobody here [in Leeds] seems to have a notion that baptism is anything more than a form of registration. I think it my duty therefore to have it always administered with peculiar solemnity.'[8]

In 1896 the Revd Hensley Henson described the common baptismal practice of his time as 'indecent in itself, discreditable to the Church, and highly injurious to religion'.[9] These concerns were minority voices in the nineteenth century, but, as the twentieth century progressed, they became more and more mainstream. In the 1960s, Baptist theologian George Beasley-Murray argued against the indiscriminate baptismal policy of other churches. He said that 'baptism, instead of being the door into the Church, has become a means of bracketing the Church and the world in a fictitious unity that enfeebles the Church, blunts the Gospel, and deceives the world'.[10]

Despite these misgivings, the policy of christening all infants presented to them, with very little preparation or inquiry into a family's faith, continued in most Church of England churches well into the second part of the twentieth century. A priest ordained in 1945, who had ministered throughout most of the second half of the twentieth century in various dioceses, described a similar picture to that observed by the Marquess of Blandford in the 1850s as still being common in the first few decades of his ministry. He told me that families simply filled in a form and turned up at the appointed time. Looking back at the first few decades of his ministry, when I spoke to him in 2014 he was dismayed at what was then normal practice; it appeared terrible in the light of later attitudes, but he said he did not question it at the time.

In some quarters, however, the appropriateness of baptizing all children presented was beginning to be questioned. In the inter-war period, the gulf between the Church's ideal of baptism as the beginning of a dedicated life of discipleship, and its use by much of the population as a rite of passage of birth, was becoming a cause for concern.

> In 1939 it was reported to the upper House of Canterbury that in the previous twenty-four years 67 per cent of all babies born in England, that is 11 ½ millions, were baptized in the Church of England, yet the Easter communicants in 1937 numbers only 2 ¼ millions. Moreover, of the 67 per cent baptized, only 26 per cent were confirmed, and no more than 9 per cent became regular Anglican communicants. It was abundantly clear that the act of Baptism initiated but did not incorporate.[11]

Others in the early twentieth century argued positively for the continuation of the practice of christening as many children as possible. Oliver Quick argued that universal baptism did not empty the rite of meaning, but rather made Christians like Christ, acting on behalf of humanity; in a similar way 'there is a sense in which all Christians are baptized ... for the not yet reborn'.[12]

Perhaps due to the increased ecumenical dialogue of the twentieth century, or to the sense that the Church needed to redefine itself as a missionary body in a largely hostile environment, these questions led to considerable debate in the 1960s about the validity of infant baptism, not just in the Protestant denominations, but even within the Roman Catholic Church. In the Church of England, Bishop Colin Buchanan published the

Grove booklet *A Case for Infant Baptism*, in which he defended the practice of the baptism of infants, but argued that the reasons only applied in the case of the children of practising Christians.[13]

This call to restrict baptism to churchgoing families became an increasingly common approach in the Church of England in the late twentieth century, especially among evangelical Anglicans. It no longer seemed appropriate to baptize all babies who were presented at church, since most babies who were christened were perceived as having 'no reasonable prospect of being brought up in a Christian environment'.[14] The trouble with this approach is that clergy then needed to work out how to decide whether or not a family were really practising Christians. Some parishes introduced tests, such as requiring a habit of churchgoing for a certain amount of time prior to the service, while others used it as an opportunity to evangelize and required parents to complete a preparation course, sometimes even a full Alpha course, before agreeing to christen their child. Those advocating such measures were often highly critical of the 'apparently indiscriminate' baptism policies common before the 1970s and still in practice in much of the Church.[15]

The 1991 Toronto Statement, from the meeting of representatives of many different Churches of the Anglican Communion, made the importance of baptism, and baptismal policy, for the churches' understandings of themselves very clear:

> There is a need for the Anglican churches to relate the administration of baptism to the reality of the reception of the gospel. The sacrament must portray God's grace as both given and received, so that a realistic visible boundary to the church on earth is established.[16]

Others, like Mark Dalby,[17] have been highly critical of the move towards more restrictive baptism policies on the grounds that they do not show the grace of God, available to all, and the injustice and impossibility of asking clergy to make a judgement about the sincerity of applicants.

These debates continue in the Church of England to this day, and represent the tensions between the two different models of church, the societal and the congregational. The work of the Life Events team represents a viewpoint that errs towards the societal end of the spectrum of ecclesiological models. The work of Colin Buchanan lies more at the congregational end, although neither is an extreme end and both seek to understand and work with others across the spectrum.

So, should the Church of England aim to be more of a sectarian or a societal church? Both ecclesiological models have precedents throughout the history of the Church, and in the teachings of Jesus, and both have positive and negative aspects. Jesus taught his followers to call God 'Father' (Matthew 23.9), and to approach him on their own, without intermediaries and without public show (Matthew 6.6). Richard Thomas has argued that this approach is seen in what he calls 'centre set' believers,[18] those who regard the Church as a resource rather than a condition for salvation, and often do not see church attendance as necessary to Christian belief. Jesus described the kingdom of heaven as being a mixture of good and bad, like a field in which the weeds are mixed with the wheat (Matthew 13.24–30); this could be used to argue that the Church can or should be a mixture of the more and less devout. Troeltsch argued that 'the Church-type is obviously superior to the sect-type and to mysticism',[19] because the very mixed-ness of the church-type churches is part of their strength: they are available to all, all can access God in their own way and on their own level, making the grace of God apparent in the unworthiness of the members. He acknowledges, however, that this openness does involve compromise on the high ideals of the faith as taught by Christ, and here we see the biblical argument for a sectarian ecclesiology. Jesus urged his followers to be perfect (Matthew 5.48) and that the law should stand and be kept in every detail (Matthew 5.18). He taught that compromise and anything less than wholehearted commitment was not enough (Luke 9.62).

The Church of England is clearly a mixture of the congregational and the societal, of sect and church, and operates in a mixed economy. The latter part of the twentieth century saw a lurch towards the congregational. However, I can see signs of some parts moving back in a more societal direction again, for example in the Life Events team and the work of sociologist of religion Linda Woodhead, and in an increasing emphasis in many parts of the Church on mission as an engagement with society, working with others of all faiths and none to improve the conditions of the poor and marginalized and to care for creation together.

The missiological challenge of living with mixed models of church

Many families who seek a christening for their child today do so because, on some level, they want them to be brought up as a Christian or to be a part of the Church, and yet they have no expectation that either of these things has anything to do with churchgoing and perhaps they may have only a little understanding of the Christian faith. Such families are carrying on a way of approaching the Christian faith that has been the norm in a communitarian church for centuries. This approach was accepted and enabled by the Church, but lived out in ordinary social life in a quiet and understated way, and often mixed in with other beliefs and practices. The Church to which such families feel a sense of belonging is a societal church, but among churchgoers it is perhaps more common to hold an ecclesiology more on the congregational end of the spectrum. This leads to clashes of expectations and misunderstandings between churches and baptism families, and so the tensions that have been noted throughout this book continue.

The difference between a Christian faith lived with little regular connection to the Church of 100 or 200 years ago and one lived today is the huge decline in the understanding and knowledge of the Christian faith in society at large. If we are to continue to be a societal church, which is open to all who live within our parishes, the Church of England needs to work out how we can be a church that promotes faith, that shares the stories of the Bible, that encourages people to engage with God, a church that offers resources to open the door to prayer and to a deepening life of faith. This may result in churchgoing, which would be wonderful, but it may not, and it is important and valuable even if it does not. The challenge to the Church, therefore, is a missional one, to open up a language of faith to the people in our communities so that those who may wish to reach out to God have the words to do so.

This missiological challenge is not one that involves attempting to persuade non-churchgoing families who seek a baptism that they are not real Christians and ought to convert and reject their previous understandings of baptism in order to see the 'true' teachings about what this means. Instead, it is a challenge to build on a foundation of faith, to fan into flame rather than to put out the smouldering wick (Matthew 12.20).

What does baptism mean to non-churchgoing families?

At the start of this chapter I asked if a christening is really what many families want, or whether a naming ceremony or other ritual would better serve their needs. The truth is that families will vary considerably. For some, the social meanings associated with the word *christening* will be the only things they are seeking, and for such families a naming ceremony, in church or in a secular setting, will be the right choice for them. However, many families will see themselves as members of a societal church, and Christianity will be an important part of their self-identity, even if this is rather vaguely understood. For such families it would surely be better to build on this, rather than to disregard it because it does not fit with our more congregational understanding of what it means to be a Christian. The social meanings associated with *christening* are not antithetical to a Christian understanding of this sacrament; they represent a good starting place for exploring the meaning of baptism. By engaging with the naming of the child at a christening, clergy can affirm the importance of recognizing the unique identity of the child within their family and society, and build on this to point to the fact that they are known by God, and in him can find renewed identity and meaning for life.

By engaging with and affirming the promises of love and commitment (marriage-like vows) that families often wish to make to a child when they are christened, clergy can talk about what fullness of life really means. To be known and loved by our families is key to this, as families will understand. They may also have a sense that they want the child to be known and loved by God, and this can lead us to dig deeper into God's plans for us to have life in abundance (John 10.10). We can talk about the unique and loved creation of each of us by God, who has made us to be people who know him, and 'our hearts are restless till they find rest in Thee'.[20]

The next chapter will ask the second of the questions posed earlier: is it really appropriate to allow those who are not committed enough to the Christian faith even to come to church regularly to contribute to what this essential sacrament means? It will ask, 'Whose Church is it anyway?'

Notes

1 Mumsnet (2013), 'To Lie to the Church about Our Godparents?' Retrieved 18.1.17, from www.mumsnet.com/Talk/am_i_being_unreasonable/1747281-To-lie-to-the-church-about-our-godparents. Parentheses added.

2 Millar, S. (2018), *Life Events: Mission and Ministry at Baptisms, Weddings and Funerals*, London: Church House Publishing, p. 34.

3 Mumsnet (2013), 'To Lie to the Church'. Parentheses added.

4 Weber, M., et al. (1973), 'Max Weber on Church, Sect, and Mysticism', *Sociological Analysis* 34(2), pp. 140–9.

5 Wright, D. F. (2005), *What has Infant Baptism Done to Baptism? An Enquiry at the End of Christendom*, Milton Keynes: Paternoster Press, p. 46.

6 Grimes, R. L. (2000), *Deeply into the Bone: Re-inventing Rites of Passage*, Berkeley: University of California Press, p. 50.

7 Hansard, HC Deb, 27 June 1855, vol. 139 cc221–37, 221.

8 Hinton, M. (1994), *The Anglican Parochial Clergy: A Celebration*, London: SCM Press, p. 255.

9 Carr, W. (1985), *Brief Encounters: Pastoral Ministry through the Occasional Offices*, London: SPCK, p. 63.

10 Beasley-Murray, G. R. (1966), *Baptism Today and Tomorrow*, London: Macmillan, p. 3.

11 Davies, H. (1996), *Worship and Theology in England: V, The Ecumenical Century 1900–1965; VI, Crisis and Creativity*, Grand Rapids, MI: Eerdmans, p. 337.

12 Quick, O. C. (1927), *The Christian Sacraments*, London: Collins, p. 169.

13 Buchanan, C. O. (1973), *A Case for Infant Baptism*, Bramcote: Grove Books.

14 Hanson, A. T. (1975), *Church, Sacraments and Ministry*, London: Mowbray, p. 51.

15 World Council of Churches (1982), *Baptism, Eucharist and Ministry*, Geneva: World Council of Churches, section 16.

16 Holeton, D. (ed.) (1991), *Christian Initiation in the Anglican Communion: The Toronto Statement 'Walk in Newness of Life': The Findings of the Fourth International Anglican Liturgical Consultation, Toronto 1991*, Bramcote: Grove Books, section 1.6.

17 Dalby, M. (1989), *Open Baptism*, London: SPCK.

18 Thomas, R. (2003), *Counting People In: Changing the Way We Think about Membership and the Church*, London: SPCK, pp. 54–5.

19 Troeltsch, E. (1931), *The Social Teaching of the Christian Churches*, Vol. 2. trans. by Olive Wyon, London: Allen & Unwin, p. 1007.

20 Schaff, P. (ed.) (1886), *A Select Library of Nicene and Post-Nicene Fathers of the Christian Church: Volume I: The Confessions and Letters of St. Augustin, with a Sketch of his Life and Work*, Edinburgh: T & T Clark, p. 45.

9

Whose Church is it anyway?

I have argued that, although social meanings of the rite of Christian initiation that are commonly associated with the word *christening* are not sufficient for a fully rounded understanding of Christian baptism, they are nevertheless a good start and can be used as a basis to explore deeper into the Christian heritage. However, the giving of a name, the introduction of a new child into a family or into society, even the giving of godparents, are not meanings of baptism that are present in the Bible or even in the early Church. These things evolved over time, as outlined in Chapters 4, 5, 6 and 7, in response to social needs of the day within Christian communities. But baptism is a dominical sacrament of the Christian Church, an essential ritual, which defines a Christian and was commanded by Christ. Can the meanings of such a fundamental rite change over time? And if so, is it right for it to evolve according to the needs of ordinary believers, many of whom have more social than religious motivations? This chapter will explore these questions.

The ever-evolving nature of religion

It is tempting to see religion as a depository of unchanging and sacred practices, texts and beliefs. Reformations and revivals often appeal to an earlier ideal and portray themselves as restoring a more pristine version of the faith, before it was corrupted by the worldliness of a church that had become too close to the interests of the ruling elite. In the past, the study of baptism has often appealed to a fourth-century ideal, encouraging modern churches to strip away the corruptions of the rite that occurred in medieval times. However, there is nothing particularly special about the fourth century: why should the changes made to the rite between its beginnings in the time of Jesus and the fourth century be acceptable, while the changes made since then are not?

All the world faiths which have known long-term success have shown a remarkable capacity to mutate, and Christianity is no exception, which is why one underlying message of this history is its sheer variety. Many Christians do not like being reminded of Christianity's capacity to develop, particularly those who are in charge of the various religious institutions which call themselves Churches, but that is the reality and has been from the beginning.[1]

Religions do change over time, this much is indisputable, but the question is to what extent this is right or helpful, and to what extent it should be resisted. For some, changes like these may seem to represent a corruption of the biblical simplicity. But the Church, throughout its history, has changed, and many of the changes, which have come about through the experience of faithful Christians adapting to the times they are in, have been accepted as part of the Christian faith. The faith needs to be reinterpreted and reapplied to each new generation; it is ever evolving. The Spirit of God can be active in religious change. Not all changes are positive, but some adaptation and evolution is necessary for a faith to continue to meet the needs of people in changing circumstances. It could be argued that religions changing in response to human needs and different social circumstances make religion a consumerist experience, morphing and changing to suit human needs. Such a consumerism in religion is in danger of emptying it of any power to challenge and inspire people, as Paul Heelas argued of the 'pick-and-mix' religion of the New Age:

> Because it does not seek an 'Other', it is incapable of transcending the limits of the self, which is idolized.
>
> No doubt there has always been a utility aspect to religious life, but for religion to be religion in any significant functional sense of the term there must be limits to the extent to which it panders to the consumer.[2]

It is certainly true that changing with the wind, making faith easy to fit in with whatever lifestyle comes into fashion at a particular time, will make that faith shallow and thin. However, a balance is needed, because a religion that cannot adapt, that is impervious to the needs of the time, will become a hardened fossil and lack all ability to touch the lives of people in the newly changed world, and fail in its fundamental purpose of forming a bridge between human beings and the Divine.

The Church is a communal body, and together it needs to decide which new directions of doctrine and practice are acceptable, and which are not. When different members disagree on what this direction should be, this can cause pain and confusion, as the Church has experienced in recent decades over issues of gender and human sexuality. Nevertheless, through this crucible the inherited religion adapts to the cultural situations in which it finds itself.

This does not need to be a question of ideal versus pragmatism, though. There are good theological reasons why an evolving community of faith should not always be regarded as one that is moving away from a fixed, divinely given norm. Change can be a process in which God is active. As a trinitarian God who exists in relationship, God is capable of working within the evolving relationships of human society. The Bible itself shows a process of change and adaptation as the people seeking after God attempt to follow the teachings handed down to them in the new contexts in which they find themselves. The incarnation is a doctrine that suggests that God himself can be fully expressed through a particular human person in a particular geographical and cultural setting, and so God can be found within human culture, as well as above and beyond it. At many stages in the Church's history, changes have been embraced as signs of the Holy Spirit's leading of the Church, as seen in the rite of confirmation and the doctrine of the Trinity, neither of which are fully formed in Scripture, but rather developed in the first few centuries of the Church's life. In the case of the Trinity, this third-century doctrine is regarded as essential to Christian faith, despite the fact that it was only fully developed after the New Testament era. Christians believe in a trinitarian God, a God who exists in community. Meanings of baptism, and other rites and practices of the faith, which are socially constructed within a community, can form part of God's creative process of meaning-making.

Religious change, like any other change, experiences push and pull factors, factors that tend to keep things the same and factors that promote change. What makes the teachings, practices, ideas and rituals of a religion sacred is the passing on and treasuring of them over time. As individuals, families and communities invest their deepest hopes, fears and yearnings in rituals, books and objects, and anything else that is held as sacred, these things become indelibly linked with sacrality. A relationship between themselves and the divine, the sacred, the transcendent, is reinforced and made real in these objects, ideas and practices as individuals and communities engage in spiritual practices such as prayer and ritual. People become caught up in a web of meaning that links heaven and earth.[3] These practices, ideas and objects are then passed on down generations within a community, and this process of handing down what is precious and sacred itself also builds this web of meaning, as a chain of memory is formed through the repetition of actions, words and beliefs.[4] However, over time, the needs of the community will change. And in changed circumstances there will be pull factors to change, to adapt the relationship with the sacred to fit in with the new circumstances, but also push factors that prevent change. It is the very act of changelessness, of passing on the precious cargo of sacrality, that makes something sacred, so a resistance to change is also essential and helpful in religious life if not taken too far so that faith becomes stagnant. For some, change will be desirable and exciting: those with little to lose, the outsiders, the poor, often the young. However, for others, who have invested in the current system as it stands, the wealthy, the powerful, but also ordinary people who have built a life based on the world as it is over many years, change will be frightening and resisted with passion. These push and pull factors will check religious change, in a similar fashion to social change, and usually cause it to go slowly so that the rate of change is usually slow enough for the chain of memory not to be broken.

However, as Danièle Hervieu-Léger argues, the changes of modern life have resulted in the fragmentation of this chain of memory. The mechanisms for passing down the chain have been disrupted by industrialization, individualism, urbanization and an increasingly mobile society. Callum Brown argues that the social emancipation of women in the 1960s was key to the breakdown of the process of passing the Christian faith on through the generations.[5] These social changes have led to the fragmentation of religion, creating a kind of 'library' from which individuals can pick up fragments of sacred ideas and weave them together to make their own spirituality or sense of the sacred. For this reason, Hervieu-Léger argues that the modern Western way of life has not led to the death of religion but rather to an 'explosion of the religious';[6] religious ideas and spiritualities have become fragmented, and people now choose from a vast and confusing array of practices, ideas, beliefs and traditions. This new religious landscape has made membership of religious bodies much more important than it was in the past, since religion is a choice, not an inherited thing that people are assumed to be a part of. In the midst of a sacred marketplace, sectarian religion makes more sense than a communitarian church. The boundaries of the Church have hardened, and both those firmly on the inside of church life and those firmly on the outside are likely to see membership in a much simpler way than people would have done in the past. You are either a Christian or you are not; the fuzzy boundaries of societal churches make much less sense in this culture of religious choice. The assumed and changeless nature of a communitarian religion, in which a shared story and belief set are taken for granted as a background to everyday life, is difficult to sustain in a modern, globalized and multi-faith world, in which contact with entirely different sets of assumptions and shared stories is inevitable. The clash between two different communitarian religions can lead to conflict and mistrust.

Nevertheless, these large-scale social changes do not happen instantly or universally; there remains a large number of people who are still on the fringes of church life, and still see themselves as Christian because of their heritage and family traditions. Christianity is much more likely to be caught than taught, because sacrality is a fundamentally shared, communitarian thing, rather than an individualized one. It is in shared ritual, mutual treasuring of ideas, people and practices, it is in everyday actions, that webs of sacred meaning are built. For this reason, there is also a tendency to maintain communitarian churches, in which faith is less individual and passionate, and more a shared backdrop, a setting in which life can be lived and which can be turned to in moments of need but may lie unexamined and infrequently acted upon in ordinary times.

And so, in modern Western culture, we remain caught between the pull towards sectarianism in our churches, between having clear boundaries and well-defined categories of insider and outsider, and the pull towards communitarianism, leading to large fringes of church life and more ambiguity in membership. Those who remain in these grey areas on the boundaries of church life are likely to be those who pick and mix from elements of Christian and other traditions. As has happened for centuries, people opt in and out of aspects of the Christian religion, while combining these with elements of other traditions from a variety of sources. Modern people who regard themselves as Christian, but who are not churchgoers, may well combine a reverence for Jesus and a belief in God, and a sporadic or even reasonably regular habit of prayer, with belief in ghosts or crystals. They may believe that their deceased family members, especially children, become angels or stars. They may anticipate a reunion with their loved ones in heaven. Or they may have any combination of beliefs and practices from a variety of Christian and other sources. In recognizing such self-proclaimed Christians as members of the Church we face both the risk and the benefit of opening up Christianity to a plurality of voices and influences. Christening has been, and will always be, a rite on the edge: it is a boundary-marking ritual, the gateway between church and world, and as such it is both a creative and an uncomfortable place for clergy and committed churchgoers.

'Insiders' and 'outsiders'

The 2011 census found that 59.3 per cent of the UK population selected 'Christian' when asked about their religion. In 2010, the Brierley consultancy found that 5.5 per cent of the population of England attended church.[7] Both these figures have declined in the years since, with the latest figure on church attendance from Brierley being 4.7 per cent in 2015, and more recent surveys finding much lower proportions of the population claiming to be Christian, usually around 50 per cent.[8] So, consistently around 90 per cent of those who see themselves as Christian in Great Britain do not go to church, or at least they don't go regularly. Is this 90 per cent mistaken in thinking that they are Christian? Or are they defective or incomplete Christians? Or, if we are to believe them, and take their assertion to membership of the Christian religion seriously, then should their views on what baptism means be considered to be valid voices in the debate within the Church about the nature of this rite?

> When we hear the cry, 'Baptism only for the children of Christian parents', we need to think carefully just what this means. In the strictest sense there is only one Christian, and that is Our Lord himself. But in another sense every baptized person is a Christian. He may be a good Christian, a bad Christian, a devout Christian, a careless Christian, but he is still a Christian.[9]

Despite the dramatic decrease in those claiming adherence to any religion, especially among younger generations, there is still a sizeable minority of younger adults who self-identify as Christian without regular church attendance, as Matthew Guest and his colleagues' investigation into the faith experiences of Christian university students has shown. They found nearly three-quarters of those students who identified themselves as Christian in the survey did not attend church regularly, and a third see themselves as Christian but have never attended church regularly (or even infrequently). They note that students from an Anglican background especially did not feel the need to attend church. Meanwhile, among those who do attend church, including Anglicans, there is a tendency for these churches to be gathered churches with clear boundaries and a strong sense of identity and difference from the surrounding culture.

> If Anglican church attendance becomes dominated by the conservative activists, the inactive Anglican majority may feel ever more alienated from their cultural Christian home. Growth in Anglican allegiance among conservative undergraduates could result in the Church of England looking less and less like an inclusive Church for the whole nation.[10]

The Church of England is increasingly reliant for funding on the congregations' giving, leading to the temptation for the needs of the congregations to take precedence over the needs of other parishioners. Through the latter part of the twentieth century, feeling its congregations dwindling, the Church placed more emphasis upon the importance of churchgoing for Christian faith. Yet, there are still many more people who claim to be

Christians who do not attend church regularly than there are those who do. What is the nature of the Christian faith that these people hold, or say that they hold? Naturally it will be very diverse; for some the faith may be a daily reality, a living relationship with God in Jesus. For others it may be a much quieter background conviction, rarely thought of or acted upon except at moments of joy or crisis. For still others it may be a distant memory, a sense of identity and belonging, with little impact on the life lived. Grace Davie famously described this group of people as those who believe without belonging,[11] because they continued to believe in God and regard themselves as Christians without attending church or having a sense of belonging to the congregational community. Alan Billings[12] turned this on its head, arguing that this group do not believe in any conventional sense in the Christian faith, beyond the existence of God and a vague sense of valuing the person of Jesus, but they did feel a sense of belonging to the Church, a sense that it was *their* Church, and that they had a right to its services, even though they did not expect this belonging to translate into Sunday attendance.

Does it make sense to describe this group as 'believers'? They certainly do not hold to a full set of orthodox Christian doctrines. And yet, as Ann Christie's study of the Christology of churchgoers shows, neither do many regular church members.[13] Slavoj Žižek's[14] idea of interpassivity may be helpful here. Parents often encourage their children to believe in Santa Claus, almost on their behalf as they are unable to believe. Christian faith may for some people be a bit like this. Those who have a sense of allegiance to the Christian faith without regular churchgoing may want to believe to some extent and/or hold a set of values that they perceive to be broadly Christian. They may want the benefits of faith and the blessings of the Divine, without feeling able to believe in the full range of Christian doctrines or wanting to commit to regular churchgoing. The idea that churchgoers and more committed Christians may practise their religion in some ways on behalf of those who want to ally themselves with the faith, but without a full commitment, is seen in Davie's later characterization of this group, as those for whom the Church maintains a 'vicarious memory' of the traditions on behalf of the non-churchgoing majority.[15] In this view, the churchgoing minority are seen by the majority as practising their faith on their behalf; churchgoing for this group is seen as a good thing for 'them' to do, but for 'us' it is something to fall back on in moments of need and for the occasional offices.

All these descriptions point to different ways of characterizing this very diverse group. They are difficult to understand properly since, unlike churchgoers, they are not usually very vocal about their beliefs or religious adherence. Its unstated nature is perhaps one of the most prominent features of their religious viewpoint. There is, however, much more to the religious and spiritual lives of people, be they churchgoers, irregular churchgoers or non-churchgoers, than their relationship with the institution of the Church, or even than the contents of their beliefs. Religion, as experienced by real people, is not neatly defined or easy to compartmentalize. Abby Day conducted interviews with people who had selected 'Christian' on the 2001 census and attempted to find out what they meant by doing this. She found that many believed that they were born Christians, that this information was on their birth certificate, and that it was a part of being British. She describes them variously as 'performative', 'nominal' and 'cultural' Christians. However, she is keen to emphasize that 'nominal' does not mean that this identity is unimportant to people. Rather, it is a deep marker of many highly significant cultural values, shared history, sense of belonging and morals. Thus, religion has not become private, as Davie's idea of 'believing without belonging' may suggest, but rather a very 'public social act',[16] a declaration of identity.

Some of the earlier attempts to characterize the religion of irregular churchgoers have come to be seen in later years as patronizing or dismissive. 'Folk religion' in particular is seen as having negative connotations. Bruce Reed used this term, along with 'secular religion', as examples of types of dysfunctional religious expression. Folk religion, in his scheme, was seen as somewhat infantile. He argued that this group keep the symbols and follow the outward rituals of Christian life, such as baptism, but do not understand the Christian message behind them.[17] As a student of theology I was discouraged from using the term 'folk religion' because of this toxic background and derogatory and patronizing tone. However, 'folk religion' simply means 'the religion of the people'. The fact that this is regarded negatively is a symptom of the fact that ordinary religion has not been taken seriously, has been denigrated and treated as insignificant. 'Folk linguistics' does not carry any of these derogatory meanings; it simply refers to what people believe about the language they use, and it is commonly used in linguistics.[18] I think that it is time to reclaim *folk religion* as a valid and interesting category, worthy of taking seriously, much as ordinary theology has begun to be. The religion of the people is important, because it is in real life that religion makes sense, where ideas are incarnated into a way of life, where a relationship with the Divine becomes transformative, and communities build a web of sacred meaning that can be passed on as a chain of memory, building meaning and significance as it is passed on.

In *Food, Sex and Strangers*,[19] Graham Harvey focuses on religion as a means of managing the boundaries between humans and other species and between people. Christening is a classic boundary-drawing event,

changing the status of the candidate from 'outsider' to 'insider'. However, different ecclesiologies, different understandings of what it means
to be church, make this distinction between 'insider' and 'outsider' problematic. If the Church is considered as consisting of all the baptized, then
in England the Church is suffering from a deep divide. On the one hand,
the minority, perhaps around 10 per cent, attend church more or less
regularly and are in some ways shaped by its language, culture, beliefs,
expectations and values. On the other hand, there is the majority, who
would describe themselves as Christian but do not regularly attend church
services. They may hold some Christian beliefs and follow some Christian
practices, and they may wish to mark the key points in their lives at the
church, but their beliefs, values and spiritual practices are formed and
influenced by a wide range of traditions within society, both Christian
and from beyond the Christian faith. This is not a divide between those
who are genuinely religious and those who are not, although there will
of course be a huge range in commitment to the Christian religion within
the group of the baptized. Rather, it is a difference of relationship with
the institution of the Church, fuelled by a different belief in what the
Church is and what it means to belong to it.

Many non-churchgoers or rare churchgoers are reliant on the Church
to be there for them to mark key events in their lives and in times of crisis,
but they may also be wary of clergy and enthusiastic churchgoers if they
place too many demands on them or make them feel guilty for their lack
of conformity. How can the Church best help such people to grow in
their faith, while not being dismissive of them or devaluing their perspectives, as has so often been the case in the past?

Wesley Carr argues that baptism does not belong to the Church but
to humanity. But if the Church is defined as all the baptized, then we
do not even need to go this far. The view of those who do not come to
church, yet seek a christening for their children, is a part of the view of the
Church, and in fact may represent the majority position. For them, this
rite is definitely a *christening*. Nevertheless, the official teachings of the
Church of England's historic formularies and official documents line up
much more closely with the meanings associated with the word *baptism*.
In the past, these two sets of approaches and meanings have more or less
peacefully co-existed as clergy were keen that all people should have the
benefits of baptism, however poorly they understood the 'true meaning'
of it. However, in the latter part of the twentieth century and since the
millennium, this closeness between the Church and the population has
been eroded, and increasingly 'the Church' is thought of as only being
those who regularly attend church services. Committed churchgoers and
non-churchgoers who regard themselves as Christian have drifted further

and further apart, leading to a sense of there being 'two Churches of England'.[20] Perhaps these two have drifted so far apart to have parted company altogether, leaving each baffled by the other and unable to connect or communicate. This leaves behind many (indeed most) of the baptized. Those who regard themselves as Christian may find themselves firmly on the outside of church life; even if they regard themselves as belonging to the Church, the congregation will often not recognize this, and clergy may regard them as outsiders and non-Christians.

One incident when I was a curate brought home to me very forcibly the reality of Christian faith to some families who do not come to church. I was due to baptize a baby from a family, but was warned that they had failed to turn up for the rehearsal and perhaps were not taking it very seriously. This was compounded when they forgot about a visit I had scheduled to their home to prepare for the baptism, and I found no one in. The team felt that they were not really interested, and were considering cancelling the christening, but I decided to give it one more try. When I met them, I found they were very young, from a working-class background, and were living a slightly chaotic lifestyle, unlike the middle-class ideal of a nuclear family unit. The baby's father was clearly the one who had been pushing for the baptism of the baby, and also wanted his girlfriend, the baby's mother (aged about 19), to be baptized, which she was willing to go along with. He explained that they had always been a Christian family, and that their faith was very important to them. He was very keen that we would include the 'proper' version of the Lord's Prayer at the service, as he didn't like these modern versions. He said that the Lord's Prayer was very important to him and he said it every night in his prayers. I had never seen them before, I was sure that they were not even occasional churchgoers, and I knew that if they had turned up at church they would not have fitted in at all. I thought perhaps he was just putting on a show for the vicar, telling me what he thought I wanted to hear. But he insisted this was very important to him, and told me he had the Lord's Prayer tattooed on his back. Before I knew it, he had whipped off his top and shown me, covering the whole of his back and beautifully decorated, a massive tattoo of the Lord's Prayer, in traditional language. Whenever I am tempted to think that only churchgoers have a real faith, I think of this young man.

In her doctoral research into the perspectives of baptism families, Gillian Hill found families who perceived themselves to be churchgoers because of occasional attendance that could easily have gone unnoticed by clergy because it was not more regular. Nevertheless, from the families' perspective, this meant that they saw themselves as practising Christians. She noted one mother who had difficulty with her baptism request, was confused about the fact that she did attend church occasionally, which she felt should carry a lot of weight, she said: 'I probably go two or three times a year which I know isn't a great deal ... but it's more than a lot of people that I know ...' This woman felt herself to be far more of a practising Christian than most of the people she knew among her friends and family because she attended church, not just for special occasions like baptism and weddings, but at other times, and it became clear that this distinction is not being grasped by clergy being approached for baptism.[21]

The chain of memory: passing on the faith in modern Britain

Carr argues that the folk meanings attached to baptism cannot be separated from the Church's interpretations, and that both co-exist and should be recognized as valid.

> Baptism is a boundary event. That of an infant is associated with the liminal act of entering the world. It is also about regeneration, crossing a boundary from one world to another, or incorporation, joining one group and leaving another ... So if we ask whose story or myth we are handling, even in the primary Christian sacrament, we have to acknowledge that it is not exclusively Christian property. They are the possession of human beings and are the church's on loan or by temporary, partial appropriation.[22]

Who has the right to define the meaning of baptism? Is its significance and practice handed down straight from heaven and defined only by the words of Scripture? Scripture is normative in the faith of the Church of England, mediated by the traditions of the Church such as the articles of religion, yet the rites of the Church are complex in the meanings and associations that Christians have when they take part in them. These meanings build up over time and are handed down, as a chain of memory, accumulating and being enriched over time as the stories and actions are repeated in different generations and in new circumstances. Jeff Astley argues that theologians must take the 'ordinary' more seriously,[23] as it is in everyday life that the meanings of the faith, passed down from Scripture through the Church, are worked out and made real. The understandings of the nature of this rite associated with the word *christening* are not secular additions to a pure, theological view of baptism, but are part of the inheritance of the Church of England's joint chain of meaning, part of the rich tapestry that makes up the place of this rite in the life of the people of God. The people, the community, in which this tapestry of meanings was woven with love and devotion, was not a non-Christian community, not a secular community, but a community of the baptized. It was a community in which people sought to live out their lives as followers of Christ, even if this looked rather different sometimes from what the Church hoped or expected of its members. It was woven down the centuries of the Church's life in England and beyond. But English society has changed; can the inheritors of this kind of folk religion still be seen as Christian in the same way as their great grandparents were?

'Christian' may once have been regarded as almost synonymous with 'British', but this is no longer the case in most parts of England. English society has reached a stage in which there are still pockets of cultural Christianity, in which being a Christian is regarded as a tribal identity, an inherited status, but this is not the case for most young people growing up today. English society no longer has the structures in place to teach a religion to the next generation. Churchgoing is at an all-time low and religious literacy is also at a very low ebb, although recent changes in the RE curriculum, which are beginning to improve religious literacy among children, may yet prove to have turned this tide, if this can be maintained in the future. But the impact of the chronically low understanding of faith among young adults and the middle aged in England today has served to make the beliefs and practices of these people who 'believe without belonging' more and more fuzzy and further removed from orthodox Christian beliefs. The present generation of mothers and fathers are the children of the baby-boomer generation who refused to hand on the traditions they had been given. Those in their twenties, thirties and forties, bringing up children and teenagers today, do not have this inheritance to pass on. The vast majority had very little teaching as children in the stories from the Bible or the basic beliefs and practices of the Christian faith. The Church of Scotland liturgy for a service of Thanksgiving describes modern Scotland as a 'primary missionary situation',[24] and this could be seen as equally, if not more, applicable to England.

A reliance on people learning the faith by osmosis within a Christian society is no longer realistic in most parts of England in the twenty-first century, when only a small amount of Christian knowledge remains in the English culture as a whole. However, although the culture is very secularized, it is a secularism formed by its Christian heritage, which fights passionately for Christian values like a concern for the outcast and those unable to stand up for themselves, those who have in the past been marginalized and looked down upon like LGBTQ people, those with special needs and even animals, for whom there is a strong moral movement to defend their rights in certain sectors of modern British culture. With some positive engagement from the Church and individual Christians, Christian values can still be found and celebrated within English culture. Christian culture perhaps lies closer to the surface of modern society than most would recognize, and a renewed effort from the churches to share the Christian faith may find fertile soil in modern society.

Symbols and rituals should be a place in which members of a community can meet and find common ground, in which difference is overcome through shared history and shared stories.

> Symbols are effective because they are imprecise. Though obviously not contentless, part of their meaning is 'subjective'. They are, therefore, ideal media through which people can speak a 'common' language, behave in apparently similar ways ... without subordinating themselves to a tyranny of orthodoxy.[25]

For centuries christenings have performed this function; the formal and theological meaning of baptism has been debated among clergy and theologians, and local communities have attached folk meanings to the rite over the years. But as the rite was essential in both groups, it was one of the few occasions that brought the vaguely Christian majority of the population into contact with the hierarchy of the Church. This encounter was an opportunity for clergy to teach the people about the more orthodox meanings of the ritual. Regular contact at rites of passage, and perhaps at Christmas and Easter, between the more-or-less faithful majority of the baptized who did not regularly attend church services, and the establishment of the Church, served to keep the folk beliefs of the majority of the population grounded, at least to a small extent, in the normative and formal theologies of the Church of England.[26]

The theological meanings associated with the word *baptism*, the formal theology, the official teachings of the Church, the passages of Scripture and liturgy that explore the rich depths of meaning of this dominical rite, act as a rock around which social meanings have collected over the centuries. Modern-day English practice of baptism is a combination of the theological and social, the meanings associated with *baptism* and taught in the churches, and the meanings associated with *christening* and celebrated in families and communities. However, this balance that has built up over the centuries of Christianity in England is under threat. The decline in churchgoing in England, and the decline in understanding of the stories and teachings of the faith, means that this deep connection is becoming weaker. While around half the population still claim to be Christian, among the younger generations this is much lower. Far more people in the generation of young adults now having children claim to have no religious affiliation than to belong to the Christian faith. Unless they are churchgoers, or perhaps were churchgoers as children, their knowledge of the faith is likely to be very limited indeed. Thus, the minority of parents today who see themselves as Christian, those most likely still to bring their children to be christened, have very little chance of keeping the tradition of christening (their operant theology) tethered to the understanding of the rite in the formal and normative theologies of the Church. We end up with a christening that is slowly losing all its foundations, and over time becoming irrelevant and emptying itself of any real content.

For this reason, although I am a fervent advocate of taking the religion of non-churchgoers seriously, and accepting the seeds of faith found in those seeking a christening, I do not think we can return to a Christendom model that baptizes all and asks no questions, and assumes that God will act in the lives of those who are baptized and one day bring them to faith. He might: God is sovereign. And yet the odds are stacked against this. We in the Church need to engage with these families and try to re-anchor the seeds of faith that they have to a deeper understanding of what the life of Jesus could mean for them today. The final chapter will explore what this may look like in practice.

Rebalancing *baptism* and *christening*

I have argued that the word *baptism* is strongly associated with serious and sober meanings – with death, with religious commitment – and is used as a metaphor for suffering in the well-used figure of speech *baptism of fire*. Meanwhile *christening* is associated with celebration, parties, joy, children and family life.

The Bible contains both elements of these in its understanding of baptism. Although not specifically speaking about baptism, Jesus describes the joy in heaven over a sinner who repents (Luke 15.7), and the Ethiopian eunuch rejoiced after his baptism by Philip (Acts 8.39). The association of baptism with the gift of the Spirit is also a clear picture of joy and celebration. On the other hand, Jesus used baptism as a euphemism for death (Mark 10.38), and Paul described christening as being into the death of Christ (Romans 6.3). Both these themes continued into the liturgies of baptism in the Church down the centuries and are seen in the Book of Common Prayer. Both rebirth and death to original sin are present in these foundational texts of the Church of England.

O Merciful God, grant that the old Adam in this Child may be so buried, that the new man may be raised up in him. Amen.

Grant that all carnal affections may die in him, and that all things belonging to the Spirit may live and grow in him. Amen.[27]

The picture given by this view of baptism is that of requiring a change in the candidate, to become something different from society, to be called out and to be holy. Ralph Keifer, describing the development in the first few centuries of the Church's life, argued that this separation of individuals from the sinful world was necessary, although he conceded that it 'condemned the Church to a quasi-sectarian existence'[28] until society began to Christianize, at which stage the focus shifted on to the 'baptism of institutions', relying on culture to teach the faith to people and requiring much less of individual Christians. The reality of Christian countries in the Middle Ages, a huge time period and a large variety of cultures, will of course have contained a wide range of religious styles and levels of commitment, so the notion that a uniform 'Christendom' in which Christianity was universally followed is problematic. Nevertheless, although the reality may have been patchy, the idea of Christendom was very important in pre- and post-Reformation England. Society was expected to be, and at some times and places actively aimed to be, a Christian society that could reasonably be expected to educate children christened in the faith. This Christendom model was the inheritance of the Church of England, and the model on which it was originally based. And so, at the time of the Reformation, there was an ambiguity in the theology of baptism. On the one hand, it was expected that society was Christian, and that babies who had been christened could be assumed to have been brought into a community in which they would, as a matter of course, learn the basic tenets of the faith. Cranmer wanted and expected all babies born in England to be baptized very soon after birth. To be English was to be Christian, even though in reality there were always a few for whom this was not the case. And yet, the liturgy talked about the rescue from a dangerous and sinful world. Where was this dangerous and sinful world, if all members of society were baptized? The Articles of Religion claimed that all who were baptized were regenerated and born again, 'whereby, as by an instrument, they that receive Baptism rightly are grafted into the Church; the promises of forgiveness of sin, and of our adoption to be sons of God by the Holy Ghost, are visibly signed and sealed'.[29] The nature of the boundaries of the community of faith, the location of the dangerous world from which people were saved, was always problematic in a Christendom situation. If all, or even 99 per cent of members of society, were baptized, and if baptism acts 'as by an instrument' to graft people into Christ, then why is this world dominated by 'vain pomp and glory' and 'covetous desires'?[30] Christendom has always been an ideal, an aspiration. Just as today most people who are baptized are not churchgoers, and many are very inactive in their application of faith to their life (and this may apply to those who go to church as well as to the majority of baptized people who do not), so the ideal of a Christian society never was and never could be fully realized. Some people will realize the potential of their baptism in a life lived closer to the teachings of Christ than others, but we are all on a continuum of sin and failure, of glory and redemption. So, how can we make sense of the mixed nature of the Church, containing both saints and sinners?

Max Weber argued that, at the Reformation, society changed from encouraging its most religiously serious and ascetic members to withdraw from society into monastic life, which was the pre-Reformation model, to encouraging them to engage more actively and passionately with the world. The drive within a Calvinistic faith to 'prove one's faith in worldly activity'[31] made this engagement between faith and everyday life more passionate and led to Protestant countries becoming exceptionally productive in economic terms. Weber was interested in the economic ramifications of this, but, if he was right, what were the effects of these changes on the character of religion and of the nature of the Church and its relationship with 'everyday life'? At first sight, one might expect this to have the effect of making religion more worldly, as the most religiously motivated people were forced to engage with the secular world and became successful in it. In the battle between the theology of baptism associated with the language of *baptism* in Early Modern England, and its practice associated with *christening*, this might have resulted in the triumph of the practical and the victory of *christening* over *baptism* as the mainstream view of this rite in the late sixteenth and seventeenth centuries. However, the reverse was the case, with the practice-orientated meanings associated with *christening* being driven to the margins of public life, associated increasingly through the eighteenth century with the lower social orders. The fact that the word *christening* became less and less acceptable to those of conservative religious tendencies, especially clergy and Nonconformist groups, led to the combination of the two types of meaning, the practice and the theory of the rite, within the one word, *baptism*, by the seventeenth century. This did not have the effect of combining all aspects of the meanings of these words in one, but rather of crowning the theoretical, logocentric aspects of *baptism* as king, and the practical and celebratory aspects of *christening* as poor relations, possibly as false religion or superstition.

By founding its ethic in the doctrine of predestination, it [Calvinism] substituted for the spiritual aristocracy of monks outside of and above the world the spiritual aristocracy of the predestined saints of God within the world. It was an aristocracy which, with its *character indelebilis* was divided from the eternally damned remainder of humanity by a more impassable and in its invisibility more terrifying gulf, than separated the monk of the Middle Ages from the rest of the world about him.[32]

Thus, bringing asceticism into the world at the Reformation did not lead to the mixture of the virtues of secular and religious life, but instead to the eradication of the idea of a godly secular world. The practical was driven out by the theoretical, and so religion lost the balance that had existed within society prior to the Reformation.

And yet, as noted above, baptism should involve both death to sin and celebration of new life, both serious commitments and joyful celebration. It is a matter that is not just for the institution of the Church to define, but for all the baptized, since it is the gift of Jesus to all his followers. And yet the role of the institution of the Church in this is significant as it provides the rock that keeps the rite tethered to the tradition. Baptism has not only got valid 'religious' meanings, as seen associated with the word *baptism*, neither can it be only about family life and an affirmation of individuals, commonly associated with the word *christening*.

> Faith and worship ought ... to be a living expression of our deepest fears and hopes ...They are most alive when they are an expression of the way people live: their hopes, fears, joys, despairs, happinesses and pains ... The church ... seems all too often to reflect the 'two dimensional preoccupation with administrative convenience' locked up in its own concerns and its own theological agenda, it ... becomes increasingly alienated from the lives and experience of the people it is supposed to serve.[33]

Conclusion and pastoral responses

For the time being, many Church of England clergy and congregations are still faced with large numbers of people seeking a christening who appear to have little other connection with the Church. How should they respond? I would argue that understanding what it is that such families want, and appreciating what is good about this approach to religion, would be a good start in responding positively and with welcome, even if ultimately a particular church decides not to offer baptism to all who ask for it. Rather than writing off the motivations of such families as shallow and self-serving, it would be good to recognize and affirm the deep love and commitment such families are wanting to show to their children, the affirmation of family life, the embrace of a traditional place for religion within their families and the joy and celebration they feel. The next and final chapter in this book will explore further the practical implications of the findings of this research for practice in the Church of England today.

Notes

1 MacCulloch, D. (2010), *A History of Christianity: The First Three Thousand Years*, London: Penguin Books, p. 9.

2 Heelas, P. (1994), 'The Limits of Consumption and the Post-modern "Religion" of the New Age', in *The Authority of the Consumer*, ed. R. Keat, N. Whiteley and N. Abercrombie, London: Routledge, p. 110.

3 Orsi, R. A. (2005), *Between Heaven and Earth: The Religious Worlds People Make and the Scholars Who Study Them*, Oxford: Princeton University Press.

4 Hervieu-Léger, D. (2000), *Religion as a Chain of Memory*, trans. by Simon Lee, Cambridge: Polity Press.

5 Brown, C. G. (2009), *The Death of Christian Britain: Christianity and Society in the Modern World*, London: Routledge.

6 Hervieu-Léger (2000), *Chain of Memory*, p. 166.

7 Brierley, P. (2015), 'Church Attendance in Britain, 1980–2015'. Retrieved 4.7.19, from http://www.brin.ac.uk/figures/church-attendance-in-britain-1980-2015/.

8 For example, British Religion in Numbers (2018), *Counting Religion in Britain, January 2018*. Retrieved 12.12.18, from www.brin.ac.uk/counting-religion-in-britain-january-2018/.

9 Dalby, M. (1989), *Open Baptism*, London: SPCK, p. 88.

10 Guest, M. et al. (2013), *Christianity and the University Experience: Understanding Student Faith*, London: Bloomsbury Academic, p. 204.

11 Davie, G. (1994), *Religion in Britain since 1945: Believing without Belonging*, Oxford: Blackwell.

12 Billings, A. (2013), *Lost Church: Why We Must Find It Again*, London: SPCK, p. xii.

13 Christie, A. (2012), *Ordinary Christology: Who Do You Say I Am? Answers from the Pews*, Farnham: Ashgate.

14 Žižek, S. (1998), *The Interpassive Subject*. Retrieved 21.6.16, from www.lacan.com/zizek-pompidou.htm.

15 Davie, G. (2000), *Religion in Modern Europe: A Memory Mutates*, Oxford: Oxford University Press, p. 36.

16 Day, A. (2011), *Believing in Belonging: Belief and Social Identity in the Modern World*, Oxford: Oxford University Press, p. 72.

17 Reed, B. (1978), *The Dynamics of Religion: Process and Movement in Christian Churches*, London: Darton, Longman & Todd, p. 108.

18 See, for example, Niedzielski, N. A. and Preston, D. R. (2000), *Folk Linguistics*, Berlin: Mouton de Gruyter.

19 Harvey, G. (2013), *Food, Sex and Strangers: Understanding Religion as Everyday Life*, Durham: Acumen.

20 Welsby, P. A. (1984), *A History of the Church of England, 1945–1980*, Oxford: Oxford University Press, p. 222.

21 Hill, G. (2006), 'Birthright or Misconception? An Investigation of the Pastoral Care of Parents in Relation to Baptismal Enquiries in the Church of England', PhD thesis, University of Portsmouth.

22 Carr, W. (1985), *Brief Encounters: Pastoral Ministry through the Occasional Offices*, London: SPCK, pp. 37, 38.

23 Astley, J. (2002), *Ordinary Theology: Looking, Listening and Learning in Theology*, Farnham: Ashgate.

24 Church of Scotland (2006), *A Welcome to a Child: Four Orders for Thanksgiving and Blessing*, Edinburgh: St Andrew Press on behalf of the Office for Worship and Doctrine of the Church of Scotland, Preface.

25 Cohen, A. P. (1985), *The Symbolic Construction of Community*, London: Routledge, p. 21.

26 Cameron, H., Bhatti, D., Duce, C., Sweeney, J. and Watkins, C. (2010), *Talking About God in Practice: Theological Action Research and Practical Theology*, London: SCM Press, p. 54.

27 Book of Common Prayer, p. 268.

28 Keifer, R. A. (1976), 'Christian Initiation: The State of the Question', in *Made, Not Born: New Perspectives on Christian Initiation and the Catechumenate*, Murphy Center for Liturgical Research, London: University of Notre Dame Press, p. 144.

29 Book of Common Prayer, p. 623, article XXVII.

30 Book of Common Prayer, p. 284.

31 Weber, M. (1930), *The Protestant Ethic and the Spirit of Capitalism*, trans. by Talcott Parsons, with an introduction by Anthony Giddens, London: Routledge Classics, p. 74.

32 Weber (1930), *Protestant Ethic*, pp. 74–5. Parentheses added.

33 Cockerell, D. (1989), *Beginning Where We Are: A Theology of Parish Ministry*, London: SCM Press, p. 4.

10

Reintroducing 'christening' to Christian approaches to baptism

This book has looked at how ordinary people in England talk about having a christening, and what it can tell us about how this ceremony has become linked in the imaginations of many to some of the deepest yearnings of families, individuals and communities.

As I began my ministry as an Anglican priest, I found that clergy and parishioners in the Church of England often struggled to understand one another when families came to a church to ask for a baptism for their child. Baptism visits often felt like an exercise in talking at cross purposes. Neither party understood the other, either in terms of the language used or in terms of the meanings and assumptions about what it all meant. I wanted to understand how we got to where we are and what a christening really means to people who show little other interest in church life. With these questions in mind, I began to look at English texts, spoken and written, formal and informal, from letters, court transcripts, tracts, books and newspapers, to transcripts of radio speech, meetings, conversations and social media exchanges, from 1500 to the present day. I used corpus-based, computer-assisted research techniques to look for big patterns, and studied more closely interesting features of how language was used to explore the meaning of baptism to British English speakers (see Appendices 1 and 2 for more details about how the research was carried out).

From the research, we have seen that this split in language has origins going back to before the Reformation. The changing fortunes of how these words were used, how often and by whom, reflected religious and social changes in English society. On the eve of the Reformation, *baptism* was used only in the Bible and in theological or theoretical discussions of the rite. The practice was described universally as to *christen*, a verb that as a noun or adjective meant 'a Christian'. The Reformation brought revolutionary ideas from the Continent, but it also brought linguistic change. Protestant-leaning people in the mid-sixteenth century were early adopters of the new English word *Christian*, and were among the first to begin to use *baptism* to refer to the practice, as well as the theory, of this sacrament. As a result, they used *christening* much less than others at the time.

In the seventeenth century, this blurring of the differentiation in use of these two words continued, and for the first time *christen* was frequently used to mean 'named', both at baptism and as a figure of speech. By this time, several earlier features of language had been lost, such as the idea that it is the godparents, as much as the priest, who are instrumental in christening the baby. By the seventeenth century, some Protestant writers were beginning to show active dislike of the word *christening*, and clergy hardly used this term at all. By the early eighteenth century there was a marked difference between the language of professionals, such as lawyers and other high-status occupations, and the language of ordinary people. People of lower social status used *christening* almost all the time, and *baptism* much less. People of higher social status also used *christening* more than *baptism*, but they used *baptism* more often than the lower-status group. The exception to this was clergy, who used *baptism* almost all the time, and *christening* hardly ever.

By the end of the eighteenth century and into the nineteenth century, this slight difference opened up into a social gulf. The use of *christening* became much more firmly associated with people of lower social status, and the official records of services were no longer books of *christenings* but *baptism registers*. To use *christening* would have clearly marked a person as of lower education and social status. By the early twentieth century even ordinary people were using *christening* less; it looked as if the word might eventually die out. But it survived in the folk memory, used and treasured among ordinary people to talk about this essential rite of family, community and religious life. And towards the end of the twentieth century, as part of a general move in the language to re-embrace informal ways of speaking, *christening* made a comeback, after centuries of decline.

An analysis of the ideas associated with *christening* shows that it was not just a word but a way of thinking about this rite that was side-lined in the centuries after the Reformation. *Christening* was the thing that god-parents did for their godchildren, it was the rite of the people, owned and practised by the people, used to serve the purposes that were important to them. It was used to acknowledge a new member of society, to incorporate them and to make clear the expectations that society, including the Church, had of them, and what they could expect from society and from God. It was used to give them a name and an identity, both marking them as an individual and also as a member of a family, community, faith and nation. Christenings were used to forge new relationships in the practice of sponsorship; to make bonds between families that had some of the features of a kin relationship, binding them together with promises of help and guidance, mostly for the godchild, but also, to a lesser extent, for the rest of the family. In the late twentieth and early twenty-first centuries, *christenings* have increasingly been about making marriage-like vows of love and commitment towards children, from their parents, their new godparents and from the wider family and community.

Today, the social split that opened up in the eighteenth century remains. *Christening* is still used more than *baptism* to describe this rite in red-top tabloid newspapers aimed at working-class people, and the reverse for the higher-status broadsheets. But, even in the Houses of Parliament, *christening* is used more and more, albeit not as frequently as the more formal word, *baptism*. On Twitter, I found that messages originating from accounts without any clear church connections used *christening* over 9 times more often than they used *baptism* (123 times, compared with 13). Meanwhile in tweets with connections to churches, *baptism* was used 24 times, and *christening* only once. In fact, in the language of clergy, and in church contexts, from the time of the Reformation to the present day, every source searched in the whole of this study showed that *christening* is almost absent from the vocabulary of clergy and church-context speech and writing. Secular sources show mixes between the two words, to differing extents at different times, for different social levels and in different genres. But church-context language used *baptism* rather than *christening* over 90 per cent of the time in every single source, for over 500 years.

Does it matter? Is it just words? I do not think so. Words are how we make sense of the world. They are the matter with which we think, the framework in which our world view is formed. As clergy, we meet with families to arrange the services that they have requested for their children, and if we are fundamentally speaking a different language to them, then we need to learn their language. The first sign of the outpouring of the Holy Spirit at Pentecost is that people of all nations and languages heard the first Christians speaking in their own languages (Acts 2.4). Mission is not about bringing people to the Church and changing them so that they speak our language, but about going out and speaking the language of the people. If we are to have any chance of being successful in helping such families to find out more about the Christian faith, to create a framework within which we can open up for them pathways that may help them to move on in the way of discipleship, then we must understand where they are starting.

Life Events

The approach to baptism of the Life Events team, spearheaded by Sandra Millar, provides a welcome change from what, in the past, has sadly often been a much less positive attitude to ordinary people's understandings of christenings. Many clergy have approached the pastoral practice of preparation for a christening as requiring families first to sweep aside the 'wrong' understandings of the rite (the meanings commonly associated with the word *christening*) before sharing the 'right' view, the traditional teachings of the Church (associated with *baptism*) and requiring people to understand and actively assent to these. A guide for families to baptism in the Anglican Church, first published in 1989, asks why people seek baptism:

> Some people, especially those of an older generation, still regard it as a social convention ... All of our friends have done it, so we must too. And understandably, it's a wonderful excuse to get the whole family together for a celebration, especially if members live at a distance from each other. The only snag is that as far as the Bible's concerned, Baptism has no special connection with family festivities or time-honoured tradition. There's no reason why we shouldn't enjoy ourselves afterwards, and there's nothing wrong with tradition in itself, but Baptism operates at a much deeper level.[1]

While this guide has been careful not to be too negative, it is clear that they believe people need to remove these false understandings of the meanings of baptism prior to receiving a true understanding.

The aspects of life affirmed through the use of the word *christening* in discourse outside the core church community, however, are not purely secular, and they are certainly not antithetical to the Christian faith. Rather, they are essential Christian virtues. The affirmation of people as children of God, the recognition of them as individuals within a family and a community, the building up of networks of love and support – these are all found within the teachings of the faith and the foundational texts of the Church of England. I have argued that a healthy approach to faith will not separate out the religious from the social, emotional or practical aspects of life. By integrating all these things, christening is acting as a holistic rite of passage, keeping together all aspects of life, integrated into a whole.

If we are to understand the Church of England as I and many of my generation have known it, we need to recognize that religion is not

simply a matter of believing a few abstract metaphysical proposi-
tions that stand shaking and vulnerable before the advance of modern
science. Religion is a way of life, involving customs and ceremonies that
validate what matters to us, and which reinforce the attachments by
which we live. It is both a faith and a form of membership, in which the
destiny of the individual is bound up with that of a community. And it
is a way in which the ordinary, the everyday and the unsurprising are
rescued from the flow of time and re-made as sacrosanct. A religion
has its accumulations of dogma; but dogmas make no real sense when
detached from the community that adheres to them, being not neutral
statements of fact but collective bids for salvation.[2]

For this reason it is imperative that in the Church's theological delibera-
tions into the nature of baptism, and in the teachings that it offers to
families, the social meanings associated with *christening* are included, as
well as the themes associated with *baptism*, in order to restore baptism to
a whole rite of passage, not stunted by a lack of connection to everyday
life.

I have argued in this book that seeing this rite as *baptism* without
christening is in danger of becoming what Roger Scruton calls dogma
'detached from the community'. In the same way, of the meanings of
baptism frequently associated with the word *christening*, most would
be equally appropriate to a naming ceremony as with the sacrament of
baptism. *Christening* without *baptism* drifts away from the anchor in
the faith from which its meaning comes. The Church needs to rebalance
its theology of the rite of initiation to include both elements. And in its
pastoral care and preparation of candidates for both baptism and services
of Thanksgiving or naming, the representatives of local churches, lay and
ordained, would do well to try to understand why this rite is so important
to families. From here, once a genuine dialogue is opened and a relationship built, it may be possible to explore some of the deeper religious
meanings of the rite and to share something of the hope of the gospel.

Practical recommendations

What difference will these findings make to my own practice, and what
would I recommend to others in ministry? First of all, as has already
been done by the Life Events team in its outward-facing websites and
literature, the Church needs to stop being afraid and dismissive of the
word *christening*, but to use it unashamedly. It has a good, Christian and
thoroughly serious pedigree within the English language, and should not

be written off as being only about the party or the gifts (which, I have also argued, should be taken more seriously).

Second, I am reminded of the importance of conducting the christening service itself in a high-quality way, one that is accessible and not dismissive of baptism families. While the desire to have the service within an act of worship is a helpful way to make connections between families and the worshipping community, some styles of worship will be off-putting to families, especially long services and communion services, from which they may feel excluded. Family and friends attending a christening are likely to include many visiting children, so having high-quality provision for children is important. This should be within the service itself, rather than in separate activities in another room, since most visiting families are not usually happy to be separated from their children in an unfamiliar setting. The Church Support Hub website, and Sandra Millar's book *Life Events*, include plenty of great practical advice and creative ideas. When conducting the service, and the preparation for the service, clergy and parish representatives will do well to bear in mind what is important about this service to families. This can be done by remembering the importance of giving a name, and making the naming of the child an appropriately solemn and significant moment. It can be done by remembering how important godparents are to families; by including them in the preparation if at all possible, by praying for them by name in the service, by offering them ways of remembering and praying for their godchild, such as giving them prayer cards or certificates. It can be done by remembering how precious the child is to the family, and affirming how precious they are to God.

Third, I am reminded that families who make contact with a church to request a christening in the modern world are doing a brave and increasingly unusual thing. This contact can and should become an ongoing relationship, and good record keeping so that we can keep in touch is essential. Such families should be invited to services (especially special seasonal services, like Christmas and Harvest), community events, and social provisions such as parenting courses, toddler groups, and so on, as appropriate. A sense that the family has a relationship with the church is essential. This is likely to be personified in a personal relationship with either clergy or a lay baptismal visiting team. Ongoing relationships with families should be based upon respect for them, offering spiritual resources to help them on their journey of faith, whether this is in the church, in another church, or not in church at all, rather than trying to get them to become 'bums on seats'.

Fourth, I have become convinced that we cannot judge a person's faith or commitment to the Christian faith by whether or not they come to church. If a person wants their child to be christened, to be committed as a member of the Church and named as a Christian, I would be in no rush to convince them that they are mistaken. Instead, in my own ministry, I would seek to understand their perspectives, what christening means to them, and use this as a starting point to offer resources to grow in their faith.

Finally, I have become convinced that there is a social and spiritual need to recognize new people and to commit them to God, and the decline in baptisms has left a gulf in the ritual life of modern English people. I would like to see churches, as well as other organizations (from local registrars to the Humanist Association), offering naming ceremonies, to meet some of this ritual shortfall for families and communities.

Naming ceremonies

Baptism has declined steeply since the mid-twentieth century. Yet, at the same time as the number of christenings has been falling, the language pattern among people in secular contexts has reflected a continued development of meanings and significance of the rite for non- and irregular churchgoers, such as seen in the emergence of the idea of making marriage-like promises of love and commitment to the child. The decline in the place of religion in the life of English society has, among some people, left a hole where the practice of religion had bound society together with common meanings and stories.

The rise in the cultural significance and use of naming ceremonies shows how, while many in English society no longer want to make the commitment to the Christian religion entailed by baptism, there are features of the social, emotional and spiritual uses of the rite that people still seek. In fact most, if not all, of the things that are associated with the word *christening* are not only appropriate to baptism, but the importance of these factors can easily be attached to an alternative ceremony, such as a naming ceremony. The giving of godparent-like adults to care for the child (although the word *godparents* may be seen as misleading if applied to non-baptismal ceremonies, the concept is still widely understood and used among families who have not chosen to have a christening), the recognition of an individual within the family and community, the celebration of the family and the giving of a name, are all features that equally work for a naming ceremony, as the British Humanist Association's website is quick to point out.[3]

The Church of England has had such an alternative service, a 'Thanksgiving service', without baptism, to welcome a child and celebrate the gift of their life, since the Alternative Service Book was introduced in 1980. But in the past, it has mainly been used for committed Christian families who either do not believe in infant baptism or wish to give children the chance to make their own choice later on in life. Or it has been used as a consolation prize for families who were deemed not to be committed enough in their faith to merit baptism. Such families are likely to feel dismissed or fobbed off and would be quite justified in feeling judged in a negative way. 'Thanksgivings' are generally not known about and are little understood among most people outside regular churchgoing circles. Millar found that parents were suspicious of the idea, seeing it as secular and possibly American, due to the linguistic associations between the service and the American festival of the same name.[4]

However, the Common Worship service of 'Thanksgiving for the gift of a child' does many of the things that families want from a *christening* and would expect of a naming ceremony. If it were called a naming ceremony, rather than a Thanksgiving, then this would be readily understood and slot into a place in the ritual system of modern Britain that is already well understood and valued. Families could invite friends to such a service without feeling they needed to explain what it was. The service of Thanksgiving, using the title of a naming ceremony, could be used to make promises of love and support to families:

> We are here today to give thanks for *these children*, with their family and friends, and to support *their* parents in their responsibilities with prayer and love ... It is God's purpose that children should know love within the stability of their home, grow in faith, and come at last to the eternal city where his love reigns supreme.[5]

In the service the child is given a name (or, rather, the name already given is acknowledged) by the parents or the 'supporting friend', who can also stand with the parents and make with them the responses to the questions 'Do you receive *these children* as a gift from God?' and 'Do you wish to give thanks to God and seek his blessing?' So, kin-like relationships, like those of the godparents, which are one of the most significant aspects of baptism for families, can be forged between children and adults, to offer guidance and support to the child and to their parents.

If both baptism and naming ceremonies were offered with a clear explanation of the differences and possibilities of each, giving parents a free choice, would some families who would not have wanted to make the commitment of baptism find having a naming ceremony attractive? It could offer a way of expressing love and commitment to a child, formally naming them and recognizing their place in their group of family and friends. The Church has certainly not found Thanksgivings to be widely attractive to non-churchgoing families, but if it were offered as a naming ceremony, and was a free choice rather than a consolation prize for families not deemed 'Christian enough' for baptism, then perhaps this may give families another way to celebrate with their local church and thank God for the gift of their children.

Conclusion

As an established Church, the Church of England has inherited a mixed model in how it sees itself. On one level, it is the Church of all baptized people, of the whole nation (as originally conceived by Cranmer), and must include all in its self-understanding. On another level, it is a confessional church, one with high standards and expectations of its members, calling them to be distinctive from the rest of society and to follow Jesus in radical discipleship. The first of these, the societal view of the Church, often sees baptism as a rite of acknowledgement of each individual, to give them a name and a place within society and within their family, and to place upon them the promises and expectations that others have of them. This ecclesiological standpoint makes a lot of sense when your view of the rite of initiation is more closely allied to the meanings found in the word *christening*.

Meanwhile, the second of these ecclesiological models, the congregational or sectarian view of the Church, sees baptism as calling people out from society to belong to the Church. It places upon them expectations of conformity to the beliefs, practices and ethics of the Church. This ecclesiology makes good sense if your understanding of the rite is closer to the meanings associated with the word *baptism*. My argument has not been that we should prefer one of these to the other, but that in being aware of these tensions we may be more mindful of the assumptions that we and others will bring to this ritual, and find more creative ways to bring the best of these two approaches together. Religion can neither be entirely social nor entirely theological. Religion is a web of meaning that is forged by and within communities as they make sense of life and encounter the divine. The Church must be firmly tethered to the rock of its foundational texts, ideas, doctrines, and most importantly to the Person of the living God, Father, Son and Holy Spirit. But this faith will only come alive if lived within the context of real life, if this doctrine is allowed to live and breathe in the everyday, grounded lives of individuals, families, communities and nations. The rite of admission into this Church must, therefore, also be both a *baptism* and a *christening*. It must reclaim all the riches of the Church's inheritance, social and theological, and yet continue to change and adapt to the new situation in which it finds itself. By reconnecting with *christening*, the Church of England stands to regain a holistic and balanced understanding of this essential rite. It may even find that this change of attitude and understanding allows local churches to make more meaningful connections with parishioners, and so be more able to find a common starting point on which to begin a journey of faith and discovery together.

Notes

1 Thomas, S. (2000), *Your Baby's Baptism in the Anglican Church*, Stowmarket: Kevin Mayhew, p. 5.

2 Scruton, R. (2012), *Our Church: A Personal History of the Church of England*, London: Atlantic Books, p. 6.

3 British Humanist Association (2017), 'Humanist Namings FAQ'. Retrieved 27.1.17, from https://humanism.org.uk/ceremonies/humanist-namings/faqs/#7.

4 Millar, S. (2018), *Life Events: Mission and Ministry at Baptisms, Weddings and Funerals*, London: Church House Publishing, p. 27.

5 Church of England (2006), *Common Worship: Christian Initiation*, London: Church House Publishing, p. 18.

Appendix 1

A note on methodology

Chapter 2 argues that language is important, and has often been high-lighted as significant for theology.[1] However, very little research has been carried out into the language used by religious and non-religious people regarding religious issues. Exceptions to this are seen in the recent PhD thesis by Roads,[2] which uses a corpus-based approach to investigate Quaker communities in the seventeenth century. Another is seen in Todd's[3] Discourse Analytical research into the language used in church Bible study groups, and Heather's[4] Critical Discourse Analysis of religious language in Christian communities.

Practical theology has highlighted the importance of using empirical research to feed into theological conversations about the significance of practices and beliefs today, but this has almost always been done using qualitative sociological research methods. However, traditional sociological methods did not seem appropriate for the questions that I needed to answer. While these may have helped me in my aim of digging down into the differences in language used between church-based groups and the wider culture, I wanted to be able to see a bigger picture than a qualitative, sociologically based research project could allow. I wanted to see how things have changed over time in the language people used, and I wanted to study the language people use when they don't know they're being researched. I discovered that corpus-based linguistic research techniques would allow me to study huge bodies of naturally occurring texts. My thesis gives those interested the details of how the research was carried out,[5] so this appendix will just give a brief outline of the methodology.

I collected texts representing different genres of writing and speech for 70-year periods from 1500 to 1914, and then studied texts from 1914 to the present day in more detail. These texts included books, pamphlets, letters, court hearings, speeches in the Houses of Parliament, news-papers, radio programmes, websites and social media. Appendix 2 lists the corpora (the plural of corpus, which means a collection of naturally occurring texts) that were used in this study.

In order to build up a picture of linguistic change, and what implications this may have for changing social attitudes and ecclesiological beliefs, I wanted to make sure that I sampled as widely as possible to avoid bias. I was very aware that, as a clergyperson in the twenty-first century, I am very much a part of the story I am attempting to tell, and I wanted to avoid simply going to look where I expected to find evidence that backed up the picture I already had. The problem, as with all empirical research, is that the more evidence one gathers, the less deeply it is possible to analyse that data and do its subtleties justice. The language used by Moretti in his study of literature is a helpful tool to conceptualize the approach of this research. He contrasts what he calls 'distant reading' with a 'close reading'[6] of texts, arguing that a distant reading allows one to gather the big picture, but one may miss the details. Conversely, close reading allows greater detail to emerge, but one may be focusing on the wrong thing and miss the wider perspective. The need to combine a close and a distant reading of texts can also be applied to a study of language. There is a danger that one 'picks the wrong cherries'[7] if a researcher relies on selecting texts for closer study, as is usually the case with qualitative linguistic studies. A combination of close reading and distant reading is helpful to avoid the pitfalls of both approaches. For this reason, and unusually in practical theology, I have used a combination of quantitative and qualitative research, and this is reflected in the use of numerical data to illustrate the story of the changing use of language in Chapter 3 of this book. This numerical data has allowed me to see the 'big picture', while a closer study of a smaller number of the texts involved has allowed more details to emerge.

The specific approach that I have used in the study of language is corpus based, which allows a researcher to analyse large bodies of naturally occurring texts (corpora), with the assistance of concordancing software, which allows linguistic patterns to be spotted. Each corpus was searched for all spelling variants of a list of 'search terms'. The search terms searched for were *baptism, baptismal, baptized, baptize* etc., and *christening, christen, christened*, etc. All occurrences of these words were logged and categorized into different types of use, as well as details of the gender, social level and religious details of the writer/speaker noted, as well as details of the text such as date, genre etc. This enabled large-scale patterns in use to be analysed. These patterns prompted closer analysis of some texts in order to make more sense of the findings on a closer reading.

Chapter 3 shows the patterns that emerged in how these words were used in these texts at different time periods and in different social groups and types of texts. Chapters 4, 5, 6 and 7 look in more detail at some of the themes that arose from this study. Appendix 2 lists the corpora used and gives details of where they came from and what texts were found in each corpus.

Notes

1 For example, look in the Bibliography for works by Macquarrie (1967), Lindbeck (1984), Milbank (1997), Nichols (1997) and Astley (2004).

2 Roads, J. (2015), 'The Distinctiveness of Quaker Prose, 1650–1699: A Corpus-based Enquiry', PhD thesis, University of Birmingham.

3 Todd, A. (2005), 'Repertoires or Nodes? Constructing Meanings in Bible-Study Groups', *Journal of Applied Linguistics* 2(2), p. 1288.

4 Heather, N. (2000), *Religious Language and Critical Discourse Analysis: Ideology and Identity in Christian Discourse Today*, Oxford: Peter Lang.

5 Lawrence, S. (2018), 'An Exploration into the Language of Baptism and Christening in the Church of England: A Rite on the Boundaries of the Church', PhD thesis, University of Birmingham.

6 Moretti, F. (2003), 'Graphs, Maps, Trees', *New Left Review* 24, p. 68.

7 Baker, P. and Levon, E. (2015), 'Picking the Right Cherries? A Comparison of Corpus-based and Qualitative Analyses of News Articles about Masculinity', *Discourse & Communication* 9(2), pp. 221–36.

Appendix 2

Corpora consulted

Summary

Period 1: 1500–70	Helsinki Corpus (HC) A multi-genre diachronic prebuilt corpus, 1500–1710. 551,000 words in EModE section of corpus.	Parsed Corpus of Early English Correspondence (PCEEC) A prebuilt corpus of official and private correspondence, 1500–1710. 2,159,132 words in whole corpus (1403–1800).	Corpus of English Dialogues (CED) A prebuilt corpus including trial depositions and witness statements, 1560–1710. 458,600 words in this section of corpus (1560–1760).	Early English Books Online (EEBO) A database of printed books and tracts from multiple genres, 1475–1680. Estimated over 1 billion words in full corpus.
Period 2: 1571–1640				
Period 3: 1641–1710				

Period 4: 1711–80	**Old Bailey Proceedings (OBP):** An online-searchable database containing records of trials at the Old Bailey, including verbatim records of statements made, 1710–1913. 127 million words in whole corpus (1674–1913).		**Ordinary's Accounts:** Part of the OBP database, this contains records of the Chaplain of Newgate Prison's encounters with those condemned to hang at Tyburn, 1676–1772. 1710–29 and 1760–79 sampled.	
Period 5: 1781–1850				**Hansard:** An online-searchable database containing records of debates in Houses of Parliament, 1803–2005. Samples taken for 6 out of every 25 years. 1.6 billion words in whole corpus.
Period 6: 1851–1914				
Twentieth century	**Brown-family Corpora:** Four mixed-genre prebuilt corpora: BLOB (1931), LOB (1961), F-LOB (1991) and BE06 (2006). 1 million words plus per corpus.	**British National Corpus (BNC):** A multi-genre online-searchable prebuilt corpus of British English sampled in 1991–4. 100 million words.	**Newspaper Corpus:** Using Nexis UK, an online-searchable database of newspapers and the archives available on the *Church Times* and *Church of England Newspaper* websites, searches were made for January of 1995, 2000, 2005, 2010 and 2015 in 6 secular and 2 church newspapers. 495,394 words in articles containing search terms.	
Twenty-first century		**Twitter:** A social media platform with the facility to perform searches for search terms appearing in English tweets for three years (2013–16). 2,249 words.		

Details of each corpus

1 Early English Books Online (EEBO)

Time periods this corpus covers: 1473–1700.

Time periods searched: 1475–80, 1500–05, 1525–30, 1550–5, 1575–80, 1600–05, 1625–30, 1650–5 and 1675–80.

Size of corpus: EEBO-TCP Phase I contains over 25,000 books, EEBO-TCP Phase II contains around 45,000 monographs. Phase I and II contain an estimated total of nearly 1 billion words (Bodleian Libraries University of Oxford, 2015). Word counts can only be estimated, however, as the collection is continually added to. As of September 2016, EEBO had approximately 132,000 titles on over 17 million pages (EEBO, 2017).

Types of texts: Published books and tracts, including literature, history, philosophy, linguistics, theology, music, fine arts, education, mathematics and science.

Corpus compiled by: Text Creation Partnership, which is a collaboration between ProQuest LLC, the University of Michigan and Oxford University. It is funded by JISC and many libraries worldwide.

Notes: This was an early pilot study for which I had not developed the full range of methodologies used in other corpora, hence only sampling some of the time periods covered. Methods had not been fully developed at this stage of the project and the full range of information collected from the other three corpora that covered periods 1–3 were not collected. For this reason, findings from this study stand alone and were not contained in the comparison of the other three corpora for periods 1–3.

2 The Helsinki Corpus of English Texts (HC)

Time periods this corpus covers: c. 730–1710.

Time periods searched: Background information searches made in Old English sections (730–1150) and Middle English sections (1150–1500). Full analysis only for periods 1, 2 and 3 (1500–1710).

Types of texts: A multi-genre diachronic corpus balanced chronologically, by genre, by region and by sociolinguistic factors. Genres in EModE section include: law, science, educational treatises, philosophy, sermons, trial proceedings, history, travel, diaries, biography, fiction, drama, correspondence and Bible.

Size of corpus: 1,572,800 words of which 551,000 are for periods 1, 2 and 3.

Corpus compiled by: Matti Rissanen (Project leader), Merja Kytö (Project secretary); Leena Kahlas-Tarkka, Matti Kilpiö (Old English); Saara Nevanlinna, Irma Taavitsainen (Middle English); Terttu Nevalainen, Helena Raumolin-Brunberg (Early Modern English). Department of Modern Languages, University of Helsinki. Distributed through the Oxford Text Archive.

3 Parsed Corpus of Early English Correspondence (PCEEC)

Time periods this corpus covers: 1403–1800.

Time periods searched: Periods 1, 2 and 3 (1500–1710).

Types of texts: Letters.

Size of corpus: 2,159,132 words in about 12,000 letters.

Corpus compiled by: Terttu Nevalainen, Helena Raumolin-Brunberg, Jukka Keränen, Minna Nevala, Arja Nurmi and Minna Palander-Collin, with additional annotation by Ann Taylor. University of Helsinki and University of York. Distributed through the Oxford Text Archive.

4 A Corpus of English Dialogues 1560–1760 (CED)

Time periods this corpus covers: 1560–1760.

Time periods searched: Periods 1, 2 and 3 (1500–1710).

Types of texts: 'Authentic dialogue', including trial proceedings and witness depositions and 'constructed dialogue', including drama comedy, didactic works and prose fiction. I only used the first two of these.

Size of corpus: 1,183,690 words in total, of which 458,600 were used (trial proceedings and witness depositions).

Corpus compiled by: Compiled under the supervision of Merja Kytö (Uppsala University) and Jonathan Culpeper (Lancaster University). Distributed through the Oxford Text Archive.

5 The Old Bailey Proceedings Online (OBP)

Time periods this corpus covers: 1674–1913 (Ordinary's Accounts 1676–1772).

Time periods searched: Periods 4, 5 and 6 (1710–1913) for the Proceedings. Two sample periods of 1710–29 and 1760–79 for the Ordinary's Accounts.

Types of texts: The Proceedings was a publication, published from 1674 to 1913, which gave detailed accounts of the trials at the Old Bailey, which was bought by members of the public. As this was a commercial publication, its format and the amount of text recorded for each trial varied over time according to the needs of the day, increasing in detail and accuracy over time. Verbatim accounts of words spoken began to be included in 1712 if they were considered particularly interesting for the readership. This increased over time and, by the middle of the eighteenth century, while still a commercial exercise, the publication began to be seen as a useful record of events by lawyers. By the late eighteenth century, public interest in the publication had waned and in 1787 it ceased to be financially viable and began to be subsidized. Control over the content, to ensure accuracy, was by now complete and coverage of trials was uniform and no longer dependent on interest in the case by the public. By the nineteenth century the publication had become an official record of trials used only by legal professionals and funded by the counties of London, Essex and Kent and the City of London. The publication ceased abruptly in 1913 (Emsley, Hitchcock et al., 2015). Also included in the website is the 'Ordinary of Newgate's Accounts', a publication from the Ordinary (Chaplain) of Newgate prison, containing the accounts of his dealings with those condemned to die at Tyburn, and biographies of their lives (Emsley, Hitchcock et al., 2017).

Size of corpus: 127 million words.

Corpus compiled by: Tim Hitchcock, Robert Shoemaker, Clive Emsley, Sharon Howard and Jamie McLaughlin, et al.

Notes: The Ordinary's Accounts produced very large numbers of search term tokens, and proved somewhat repetitive in their format and tendency to use these words to preach to prisoners about how they had failed to live up to the promises made at Christian initiation because of their crimes. The quantity of material was too great to study the whole period, so two 20-year periods at the beginning and end of period 4 were selected, allowing samples from different chaplains and at different times to be considered.

6 Hansard 1803–2005

Time periods this corpus covers: 1803–2005.

Time periods searched: 1810–15, 1835–40, 1860–5, 1885–90, 1910–15, 1935–40, 1960–5, 1985–90.

Types of texts: Official reports of the debates in Parliament, both the House of Commons and the House of Lords.

Size of corpus: 7.6 million speeches, 1.6 billion words.

Corpus compiled by: Millbank Systems. UK Parliament, Commons and Lords Libraries.

Notes: The corpus produced too much material to be logged in full, so 6-year periods every 25 years were selected, beginning in 1810.

7 BLOB, LOB F-LOB and BE06

These four corpora are from the Brown Family of corpora. All Brown Family corpora contain a carefully balanced set of samples with the same number of words for each genre, as shown below. Each corpus in this family comes from a single time period and type of English, allowing comparison between time periods and types of English. These four are all for British English.

Time periods these corpora cover:
BLOB: 1931.
LOB (the Lancaster-Oslo/Bergen Corpus): 1961.
F-LOB (Freiburn-LOB): 1991.
BE06 (British English 2006): 2006.

Types of texts: Samples of over 2,000 words (number of samples of each genre in brackets) are included from the following genres for all Brown Family corpora, including these four corpora:
A Press reportage (44).
B Press editorials (27).
C Press reviews (17).
D Religion (17).
E Skills, trades and hobbies (36).
F Popular lore (48).
G Biographies and essays (75).
H Miscellaneous (reports, official documents) (30).
I Science (academic prose) (80).

J   General fiction (29).
K   Mystery and detective fiction (24).
L   Science fiction (6).
M   Western and adventure fiction (29).
N   Romantic fiction (29).
O   Humour (9).

Size of corpora: 1 million + words per corpus.

Corpus references:
BLOB: Leech, G. and Smith, N. (2005), 'Extending the Possibilities of Corpus-based Research on English in the Twentieth Century: A Prequel to LOB and FLOB', *ICAME Journal* 29, pp. 83–98.
LOB: The LOB Corpus, original version (1970–8), compiled by Geoffrey Leech, Lancaster University, Stig Johansson, University of Oslo (project leaders), and Knut Hofland, University of Bergen (head of computing).
F-LOB: The Freiburg-LOB Corpus ('F-LOB') (original version), compiled by Christian Mair, Albert-Ludwigs-Universität Freiburg.
BE06: Baker, P. (2009), 'The BE06 Corpus of British English and Recent Language Change', *International Journal of Corpus Linguistics* 14(3), pp. 312–37.

8 British National Corpus (BNC)

Time periods this corpus covers: 1991–4.

Types of texts: A synchronic corpus, comprised of a variety of samples of spoken and written texts. Ninety per cent of the corpus consists of written samples, for example extracts from regional and national newspapers, specialist periodicals and journals, academic books and popular fiction, published and unpublished letters, memoranda and school and university essays. The remaining 10 per cent consists of transcriptions of speech, both formal and informal, scripted and unscripted, private and public, for example sermons, meetings and radio transcripts and recorded conversations. The transcribed conversations are balanced according to age, gender, social class and regions (British National Corpus Consortium, 2009).

Size of corpus: 100 million words, of which I mainly used the spoken part (10 million words).

Corpus compiled by: British National Corpus Consortium. I used the Brigham Young University interface to search the British National Corpus (Davies, 2004).

9 Newspapers

Time periods searched: January of 1995, 2000, 2005, 2010 and 2015.

Types of texts: In order to gain a social balance, I searched in two broadsheet newspapers and their Sunday sister publications (*The Guardian*, *The Times*, *The Observer* and *Sunday Times*, all available on Nexis UK for all time periods). Two 'red-top' tabloids (*The Sun*, *Daily Mirror* and *Sunday Mirror* were not available on Nexis in 1995, but were for all later time periods). Also, two middle-market tabloid newspapers (*Daily Mail* and *Mail on Sunday*, which were available for all time periods, *and Sunday Express*, which was available from 2000 onwards). Two church newspapers (*Church Times*, which was available for all time periods, and *Church of England Newspaper*, which was only available to search in 2015). The secular newspapers were accessed through Nexis UK, and the Church newspapers through their website archives.

Size of corpus: The corpus size was calculated as the total number of words in articles that were studied because they contained one of the search terms, an approach used for newspaper corpus analysis by Gabrielatos and Baker (2008). The following two tables give the number of words by year (just January of these years was searched), and also by type of publication. The corpus had 495,394 words in 557 articles. These were fairly evenly spread over the years studied, with the exception of 1995, for which *The Sun*, *Sunday Express*, *The Mirror* and *Sunday Mirror* were not available on Nexis, making this year poorly represented in the corpus. This contributes to the smaller proportion of the corpus for middle-market and red-top tabloids seen in the third of these tables. However, it was only for 1995 that these papers were not available, so the difference is also due to the search terms appearing less in these newspapers, compared with broadsheets, and due to the articles containing these search terms being shorter, especially in the red-top tabloids.

APPENDIX 2: CORPORA CONSULTED

Year	Number of words in corpus	% of corpus	Number of articles
1995	53794	11	58
2000	122455	25	121
2005	118662	24	132
2010	107115	22	136
2015	93368	19	110
Total	495394		557

Newspaper	Number of words in corpus	% of corpus	Number of articles
Church of England Newspaper	6646	1	13
Church Times	53008	11	76
The Times and Sunday Times	120614	24	139
The Guardian and The Observer	124686	25	107
Daily Mail and Mail on Sunday	99269	20	80
Sunday Express	9602	2	14
Mirror and Sunday Mirror	41734	8	66
Sun	39835	8	62
Total	495394		557

Newspaper group	Number of words in corpus	% of corpus	Number of articles
Church Press	59654	12	89
Broadsheet	245300	50	246
Middle-market tabloid	108871	22	94
Red-top tabloid	81569	16	128
Total	495394		557

Corpus accessed at: Nexis (UK), *Church Times* archives and *Church of England Newspaper*'s website.

10 Twitter

Time periods this corpus covers: 2006–present day.

Time periods searched: 12 April 2013–12 April 2016, just for tweets originating in England. This was from the date the study began going back three years.

Types of texts: Micro-blogging social media messages of less than 140 characters.

Size of corpus: The corpus size consists of all tweets originating in England in the three years studied, which included one of the search terms studied (*bapt-* or *christen-* words). This gave 2,249 words over 166 tweets.

Corpus compiled by: Sarah Lawrence using texts on the Twitter website.

Notes: Due to Twitter's terms of service, in order to protect the privacy of users, it is not possible to reproduce or quote from these tweets or to pass on datasets developed from Twitter to any other people. I have used Twitter's site to access tweets that fulfil my search criteria, and have analysed this data for patterns, but I have not quoted from these tweets directly, and my dataset is not available for sharing with any third parties. See https://dev.twitter.com/overview/terms/agreement-and-policy for Twitter's terms of service.

Bibliography

Corpora (in order listed in Appendix 2)

Text Creation Partnership (2003), *Early English Books Online*, Retrieved 19.4.15, from http://eebo.chadwyck.com/home.

Rissanen, M. (Project leader), L. Kahlas-Tarkka, M. Kilpiö (Old English); S. Nevanlinna, I. Taavitsainen (Middle English); T. Nevalainen, H. Raumolin-Brunberg (Early Modern English) (1991), *The Helsinki Corpus of English*, Department of Modern Languages, University of Helsinki. Distributed through the Oxford Text Archive.

Nevalainen, T., Raumolin-Brunberg, H., Keränen, J., Nevala, M., Nurmi, A. and Palander-Collin, M., with additional annotation by Ann Taylor (2006), *Parsed Corpus of Early English Correspondence, text version*, University of Helsinki and University of York. Distributed through the Oxford Text Archive.

Kytö, M. (Uppsala University) and Culpeper, J. (Lancaster University) (2006), *A Corpus of English Dialogues 1560–1760*. Distributed through the Oxford Text Archive.

Hitchcock, T., Shoemaker, R., Emsley, C., Howard, S. and McLaughlin, J., et al. (2012), *Old Bailey Proceedings Online, 1674–1913*, version 7.0. Retrieved 26.1.16, from www.oldbaileyonline.org.

UK Parliament, *HANSARD 1803–2005*. Retrieved 24.5.16, from http://hansard.millbanksystems.com/.

Leech, G. and Smith, N. (2005), 'Extending the Possibilities of Corpus-based Research on English in the Twentieth Century: A Prequel to LOB and FLOB', *ICAME Journal* 29, pp. 83–98.

Leech, G. (Lancaster University), Johansson, S. (University of Oslo) and Hofland, K. (University of Bergen) (1970–8), *The LOB Corpus* (original version).

Mair, C., Ludwigs, A. (Universität Freiburg), *The Freiburg-LOB Corpus ('F-LOB')* (original version).

Baker, P. (2009), 'The BE06 Corpus of British English and Recent Language Change', *International Journal of Corpus Linguistics* 14(3), pp. 312–37.

British National Corpus Consortium (2009), *British National Corpus*. Retrieved 10.2.16, from www.natcorp.ox.ac.uk/.

LexisNexis (2000), Nexis UK (electronic resource), London: LexisNexis Group.

Church Times (2016), 'The Church Times Archive: 1863–Today'. Retrieved 14.5.16, from www.churchtimes.co.uk.

Church of England Newspaper (2016). Retrieved 14.5.2016, from www.church-newspaper.com/.

Twitter (2006). Retrieved 14.5.16, from www.twitter.com.

Other books and websites

9Dot Research (2013), *Christening Matters Research Report*, Kettering: Church of England.

A Bit of Fry and Laurie (1989), 'Christening', BBC. Retrieved 8.2.18, from http://abitoffryandlaurie.co.uk/sketches/christening.

Aldrin, E. (2016), 'Names and Identity', in C. Hough and D. Izdebska (eds), *The Oxford Handbook of Names and Naming*, Oxford: Oxford University Press, pp. 382–94.

Allan, G. (1996), *Kinship and Friendship in Modern Britain*, Oxford: Oxford University Press.

Archbishops' Council (2015), *The Importance of Godparents*, Church Support Hub. Retrieved 24.1.17, from https://churchsupporthub.org/baptisms/explore-thinking/importance-godparents/.

Archbishops' Council (2015), *Christian Initiation – Additional Baptism Texts in Accessible Language*, London: Church House Publishing. Retrieved 23.4.19, from www.churchofengland.org/prayer-and-worship/worship-texts-and-resources/common-worship/christian-initiation/christian.

Astley, J. (2002), *Ordinary Theology: Looking, Listening and Learning in Theology*, Farnham: Ashgate.

Astley, J. (2004), *Exploring God-talk: Using Language in Religion*, London: Darton, Longman & Todd.

Austin, J. L. (1976), *How to Do Things with Words*, 2nd edn, Oxford: Clarendon Press.

Bailey, E. (1990), 'The Implicit Religion of Contemporary Society: Some Studies and Reflections', *Social Compass* 37(4), pp. 483–97.

Baillie, J. (1964), *Baptism and Conversion*, Oxford: Oxford University Press.

Baker, P. and Levon, E. (2015), 'Picking the Right Cherries? A Comparison of Corpus-based and Qualitative Analyses of News Articles about Masculinity', *Discourse & Communication* 9(2), pp. 221–36.

Barthes, R. and Howard, R. (1986), *The Rustle of Language*, Oxford: Basil Blackwell.

BBC (1991), *Only Fools and Horses*, 'Damien's Christening, extract from Miami Twice', Part 1. Retrieved 15.12.16, from www.youtube.com/watch?v=Tx65lSH-wJFk.

Beasley-Murray, G. R. (1966), *Baptism Today and Tomorrow*, London: Macmillan.

Bertrand, M. and Mullainathan, S. (2003), 'Are Emily and Greg More Employable than Lakisha and Jamal? A Field Experiment on Labor Market Discrimination', *National Bureau of Economic Research Working Paper Series*, no. 9873.

Billings, A. (2004), *Secular Lives, Sacred Hearts: The Role of the Church in a Time of No Religion*, London: SPCK.

Billings, A. (2013), *Lost Church: Why We Must Find It Again*, London: SPCK.

Bowlby, J. (2005), *A Secure Base: Clinical Applications of Attachment Theory*, London: Routledge.

Brierley, P. (2015), 'Church Attendance in Britain, 1980–2015'. Retrieved 4.7.19, from www.brin.ac.uk/figures/church-attendance-in-britain-1980-2015/.

British Humanist Association (2017), 'Humanist Namings FAQ'. Retrieved 27.1.17, from https://humanism.org.uk/ceremonies/humanist-namings/faqs/#7.

British Religion in Numbers (2018), 'Counting Religion in Britain, January 2018'. Retrieved 12.12.18, from www.brin.ac.uk/counting-religion-in-britain-january-2018/.

Brown, A. and Woodhead, L. (2016), *That was the Church, that was: How the Church of England Lost the English People*, London: Bloomsbury Continuum.

Brown, C. G. (2009), *The Death of Christian Britain: Christianity and Society in the Modern World*, London: Routledge.

Buchanan, C. (1973), *A Case for Infant Baptism*, Bramcote: Grove Books.

Buchanan, C. (1980), 'Initiation Services', in C. Buchanan, T. Lloyd and H. Miller (eds), *Anglican Worship Today: Collins Illustrated Guide to the Alternative Service Book 1980*, London: Collins, pp. 152–82.

Buchanan, C. (1992), *Infant Baptism in the Church of England: A Guide to the Official Position of the Church in its Formularies*, Nottingham: Grove Books.

Cameron, A., Amos, A. C., Healey, A. d. and Holland, J. (2007), *Dictionary of Old English: A to G online*, Toronto, Dictionary of Old English Project. Retrieved 15.3.15, from http://tapor.library.utoronto.ca/doe/index.html.

Cameron, H., Bhatti, D., Duce, C., Sweeney, J. and Watkins, C. (2010), *Talking about God in Practice: Theological Action Research and Practical Theology*, London: SCM Press.

Carr, W. (1985), *Brief Encounters: Pastoral Ministry through the Occasional Offices*, London: SPCK.

Christie, A. (2012), *Ordinary Christology: Who Do You Say I Am? Answers from the Pews*, Farnham: Ashgate.

Church of England (1662), *The Book of Common Prayer and the Administration of the Sacraments according to the use of the Church of England*, Standard edition, Cambridge: Cambridge University Press.

Church of England (1928), *The Book of Common Prayer with the Additions and Deviations Proposed in 1928*, London: Society for Promoting Christian Knowledge.

Church of England (1980), *The Alternative Service Book 1980, together with the Liturgical Psalter*, London: Hodder & Stoughton.

Church of England (1995), *On the Way: Towards an Integrated Approach to Christian Initiation*, London: Church House Publishing.

Church of England (2006), *Common Worship: Christian Initiation*, London: Church House Publishing.

Church of England (2016), *Canons of the Church of England*, 7th edn. Retrieved 4.7.19, from www.churchofengland.org/more/policy-and-thinking/canons-church england/section-b.

Church of England (2018), *Pastoral Guidance for Use in Conjunction with the Affirmation of Baptismal Faith in the Context of Gender Transition*. Retrieved 3.7.19, from https://www.churchofengland.org/sites/default/files/2018-12/Pastoral%20Guidance-Affirmation-Baptismal-Faith.pdf.

Church of England (2019), 'Is a "Baptism" Different to a "Christening"?' Retrieved 4.7.19, from https://churchofenglandchristenings.org/for-parents/is-a-baptism-different-to-a-christening/.

Church of Scotland (2006), *A Welcome to a Child: Four Orders for Thanksgiving and Blessing*, Edinburgh, Saint Andrew Press on behalf of the Office for Worship and Doctrine of the Church of Scotland.

Cockerell, D. (1989), *Beginning Where We Are: A Theology of Parish Ministry*, London: SCM Press.

Cohen, A. P. (1985), *The Symbolic Construction of Community*, London: Routledge.

Corson, D. (1985), *The Lexical Bar*, Oxford: Pergamon.

Crockett, A. and Voas, D. (2006), 'Generations of Decline: Religious Change in 20th-Century Britain', *Journal for the Scientific Study of Religion* 45(4), pp. 567–84.

Cromie, R. and Grose, F. (eds) (1811), *1811 Dictionary of the Vulgar Tongue: A dictionary of buckish slang, university wit and pickpocket eloquence unabridged from the original 1811 edition with a foreword by Robert Cromie*, Northfield: Digest Books.

Culpeper, J. (2015), *History of English*, 3rd edn, London: Routledge, Taylor and Francis.

Dalby, M. (1989), *Open Baptism*, London: SPCK.

Davie, G. (1994), *Religion in Britain since 1945: Believing without Belonging*, Oxford: Blackwell.

Davie, G. (2000), *Religion in Modern Europe: A Memory Mutates*, Oxford: Oxford University Press.

Davies, H. (1996), *Worship and Theology in England: V, The Ecumenical Century 1900–1965; VI, Crisis and Creativity*, Grand Rapids, MI: Eerdmans.

Day, A. (2011), *Believing in Belonging: Belief and Social Identity in the Modern World*, Oxford: Oxford University Press.

De Botton, A. (2012), *Religion for Atheists: A Non-Believer's Guide to the Uses of Religion*, London: Hamish Hamilton.

Diocese of Rochester (2015), 'Top 10 Facts about Christenings'. Retrieved 4.7.19, from www.rochester.anglican.org/communications/news-in-brief/top-10-facts-about-christenings.php.

Earey, M., Lloyd, T. and Tarrant, I. (2007), *Connecting with Baptism: A Practical Guide to Christian Initiation Today*, London: Church House Publishing.

Emmelhainz, C. (2013), 'Naming a New Self: Identity Elasticity and Self-Definition in Voluntary Name Changes', *Names* 60(3), pp. 156–65.

Fisher, J. D. C. (1965), *Christian Initiation: Baptism in the Medieval West: A Study in the Disintegration of the Primitive Rite of Initiation*, London: SPCK.

Freud, S., Strachey, J., Freud, A., Strachey, A. and Tyson, A. (2001), *The Standard Edition of the Complete Psychological Works of Sigmund Freud. Volume XVII: An Infantile Neurosis and Other Works*, London: Vintage.

Gilliat-Ray, S. (2005), '"Sacralising" Sacred Space in Public Institutions: A Case Study of the Prayer Space at the Millennium Dome', *Journal of Contemporary Religion* 20(3), pp. 357–72.

Grimes, R. L. (2000), *Deeply into the Bone: Re-inventing Rites of Passage*, Berkeley: University of California Press.

Guest, M. et al. (2013), *Christianity and the University Experience: Understanding Student Faith*, London: Bloomsbury Academic.

Halliday, M. A. K. (1976), 'Anti-Languages', *American Anthropologist* 78(3), pp. 570–84.

Hanson, A. T. (1975), *Church, Sacraments and Ministry*, London: Mowbrays.

Harvey, G. (2013), *Food, Sex and Strangers: Understanding Religion as Everyday Life*, Durham: Acumen.

Harvey, L. (2012), 'How Serious is it Really? The Mixed Economy and the Light-hearted Long Haul', in G. Cray and I. Mobsby (eds), *Fresh Expressions of Church and the Kingdom of God*, Norwich: Canterbury Press, pp. 95–105.

Heather, N. (2000), *Religious Language and Critical Discourse Analysis: Ideology and Identity in Christian Discourse Today*, Oxford: Peter Lang.

Heelas, P. (1994), 'The Limits of Consumption and the Post-modern "Religion" of the New Age', in *The Authority of the Consumer*, ed. R. Keat, N. Whiteley and N. Abercrombie, London: Routledge, pp. 102–15.

Hervieu-Léger, D. (2000), *Religion as a Chain of Memory*, trans. by Simon Lee, Cambridge: Polity Press.

Hill, G. (2006), 'Birthright or Misconception? An Investigation of the Pastoral Care of Parents in Relation to Baptismal Enquiries in the Church of England', PhD thesis, University of Portsmouth.

Hinton, M. (1994), *The Anglican Parochial Clergy: A Celebration*, London: SCM Press.

Holeton, D. (ed.) (1991), *Christian Initiation in the Anglican Communion: The Toronto Statement 'Walk in Newness of Life': The Findings of the Fourth International Anglican Liturgical Consultation, Toronto 1991*, Bramcote: Grove Books.

Hornsby-Smith, M. P. et al. (1985), 'Common Religion and Customary Religion: A Critique and a Proposal', *Review of Religious Research* 26(3), pp. 244–52.

Hunston, S. (2002), *Corpora in Applied Linguistics*, Cambridge: Cambridge University Press.

Jenkins, T. (1999), *Religion in English Everyday Life: An Ethnographic Approach*, Oxford: Berghahn Books.

Jewish Telegraphic Agency (1938), 'Reich Publishes List of "Jewish Names" Barred to "Aryans"'. Retrieved 3.7.17, from www.jta.org/1938/08/24/archive/reich-publishes-list-of-jewish-names-barred-to-aryans.

Johnson, M. E. (2007), *The Rites of Christian Initiation: Their Evolution and Interpretation*, Collegeville, MN: Liturgical Press.

Joyce, P. (1991), 'The People's English: Language and Class in England *c.* 1840–1920', in P. Burke and R. Porter (eds), *Language, Self, and Society: A Social History of Language*, Cambridge: Polity Press, pp. 154–90.

Keifer, R. A. (1976), 'Christian Initiation: The State of the Question', in *Made, Not Born: New Perspectives on Christian Initiation and the Catechumenate*, Murphy Center for Liturgical Research, London: University of Notre Dame Press, pp. 138–51.

Kuhrt, S. (2009), *Church Growth through the Full Welcome of Children: The 'Sssh Free Church'*, Cambridge: Grove Books.

Labov, W. (1990), 'The Intersection of Sex and Social Class in the Course of Linguistic Change', *Language Variation and Change* 2, pp. 205–54.

Lakin, N. (2015), 'Church Needs to "Catch Up" as Vicar Urges Gender Debate', *Lancaster Guardian*, 4 June 2015. Retrieved 2.12.15, from www.lancasterguardian.co.uk/news/local/church-needs-to-catch-up-as-vicar-urges-gender-debate-1-7293295#ixzz3tAWgPC53.

Lawrence, S. (2018), 'An Exploration into the Language of Baptism and Christening in the Church of England: A Rite on the Boundaries of the Church', PhD thesis, University of Birmingham.

League of Nations (1924), 'Geneva Declaration of the Rights of the Child', United Nations. Retrieved 6.2.17, from www.un-documents.net/gdrc1924.htm.

Lerer, S. (2007), *Inventing English: A Portable History of the Language*, New York: Columbia University Press.

Lieberson, S. and Bell, E. O. (1992), 'Children's First Names: An Empirical Study of Social Taste', *American Journal of Sociology* 98(3), pp. 511–54.

Lindbeck, G. A. (1984), *The Nature of Doctrine: Religion and Theology in a Post-liberal Age*, London: SPCK.

Liturgical Commission (2014), *Christian Initiation: Additional Texts in Accessible Language*. Retrieved 8.5.14, from www.churchofengland.org/media/1903641/baptism%20pack%20for%20trial%20use.pdf. (No longer available online.)

Loewenstein, J., Basu, A., Knox, D. and Pentecost, S. (2013), 'EEBO N-gram Browser', in 'Early Modern Print: Text Mining Early Printed English', Humanities Digital Workshop at Washington University in St Louis. Retrieved 1.2.17, from http://earlyprint.wustl.edu/.

Louw, B. (1993), 'Irony in the Text or Insincerity in the Writer? The Diagnostic Potential of Semantic Prosodies', in M. Baker, G. Francis, E. Tognini-Bonelli and J. M. Sinclair (eds), *Text and Technology: In Honour of John Sinclair*, Philadelphia: J. Benjamins Pub. Co., pp. 157–76.

Luckmann, T. (1967), *The Invisible Religion: The Problem of Religion in Modern Society*, New York: Macmillan.

Lynch, G. (2012), *The Sacred in the Modern World: A Cultural Sociological Approach*, Oxford: Oxford University Press.

Lynch, J. (1986), *Godparents and Kinship in Early Medieval Europe*, Princeton: Princeton University Press.

MacCulloch, D. (2010), *A History of Christianity: The First Three Thousand Years*, London: Penguin Books.

Macquarrie, J. (1967), *God-Talk: An Examination of the Language and Logic of Theology*, London: SCM Press.

Mahlberg, M. (2014), 'Corpus Stylistics', in M. Burke (ed.), *The Routledge Handbook of Stylistics*, London: Routledge, pp. 378–92.

Maslanka, C. W. (2012), 'Christening Women, Men, and Monsters: Images of Baptism in Middle English Hagiography and Romance', PhD thesis, University of Wisconsin-Madison.

McGuire, M. B. (2008), *Lived Religion: Faith and Practice in Everyday Life*, Oxford: Oxford University Press.

McKee, D. and McKee, H. (2011), 'The Christening Song with Lyrics', YouTube. Retrieved 24.1.17, from www.youtube.com/watch?v=0frz077L2fg.

Milbank, J. (1997), *The Word Made Strange: Theology, Language, Culture*, Oxford: Blackwell.

Millar, S. (2014), 'Christening or Baptism?' Church Support Hub Website, Church of England. Retrieved 13.6.17, from https://churchsupporthub.org/article/christening-baptism/.

Millar, S. (2018), *Life Events: Mission and Ministry at Baptisms, Weddings and Funerals*, London: Church House Publishing.

Minkova, D. and Stockwell, R. (2009), *English Words: History and Structure*, 2nd edn, Cambridge: Cambridge University Press.

Moretti, F. (2003), 'Graphs, Maps, Trees', *New Left Review* (24), pp. 67–93.

Mothercare (2016), 'Christening & Naming Day Gifts'. Retrieved 10.2.17, from www.mothercare.com/gift/shop-by-occasion/christening-and-naming-day-gifts/.

Mumsnet (2013), 'To Lie to the Church about Our Godparents?' Retrieved 18.1.17, from www.mumsnet.com/Talk/am_i_being_unreasonable/1747281-To-lie-to-the-church-about-our-godparents.

Nevalainen, T. (2000), 'Early Modern English Lexis and Semantics', in R. Lass (ed.), *The Cambridge History of the English Language*, Cambridge: Cambridge University Press, pp. 332–458.

Nichols, K. (1997), *Refracting the Light: Learning the Languages of Faith*, Dublin: Lindisfarne Books.

Niedzielski, N. A. and Preston, D. R. (2000), *Folk Linguistics*, Berlin: Mouton de Gruyter.

Noble, T., Wycliffe, J. and Purvey, J. (2012), *Wycliffe's Bible: A Modern-Spelling Edition of the 14th Century Middle English Translation by John Wycliffe and John Purvey, with an Introduction by Terence P. Noble*, Vancouver: Terence P. Noble.

Northcott, M. (2000), 'Pastoral Theology and Sociology', in J. Woodward and S. Pattison (eds), *The Blackwell Reader in Pastoral and Practical Theology*, Oxford: Blackwell, pp. 151–63.

Novel Entertainment Limited (2011), *Horrid Henry and the Christening Crisis*, based on the books by Francesca Simon, illustrated by Tony Ross and published by Orion Books. Retrieved 15.12.16, from www.youtube.com/watch?v=PxWtNBK-Bxs&t=209s.

OED Online (2016), *Oxford English Dictionary*, Oxford University Press. Retrieved 23.1.17, from www.oed.com.

Orsi, R. A. (2005), *Between Heaven and Earth: The Religious Worlds People Make and the Scholars Who Study Them*, Oxford: Princeton University Press.

Owen, C. (1991), *Baptise Every Baby? The Story of One Vicar's Struggle to Treat Baptism as if it Mattered*, Eastbourne: Marc.

Pascual, A., Guéguen, N., Vallée, B., Lourel, M. and Cosnefroy, O. (2015), 'First Name Popularity as Predictor of Employability', *Names* 63(1), pp. 30–6.

Pattison, S. (2000), 'Some Straw for the Bricks: A Basic Introduction to Theological Reflection', in J. Woodward and S. Pattison (eds), *The Blackwell Reader in Pastoral and Practical Theology*, Oxford: Blackwell, pp. 135–45.

Pattison, S. (2007), *Seeing Things: Deepening Relations with Visual Artefacts*, London: SCM Press.

Penn, J. M. (1972), *Linguistic Relativity Versus Innate Ideas: The Origins of the Sapir-Whorf Hypothesis in German Thought*, The Hague: Mouton.

Perl, P. and Wiggins, J. L. (2004), 'Don't Call Me Ishmael: Religious Naming among Protestants and Catholics in the United States', *Journal for the Scientific Study of Religion* 43(2), pp. 209–28.

Piaget, J. (1968), *Structuralism*, trans. by Chaninah Maschler, London: Routledge & Kegan Paul.

Pope Benedict XVI (2011), 'Feast of the Baptism of the Lord', Rome: Vatican. Retrieved 16.12.16, from http://w2.vatican.va/content/benedict-xvi/en/angelus/2011/documents/hf_ben-xvi_ang_20110109_battesimo.html.

Prickett, S. (2009), *Modernity and the Reinvention of Tradition: Backing into the Future*, Cambridge: Cambridge University Press.

Quick, O. C. (1927), *The Christian Sacraments*, London: Collins.

Reardon, M. (1991), *Christian Initiation: A Policy for the Church of England: A Discussion Paper*, London: Church House Publishing.

Reed, B. (1978), *The Dynamics of Religion: Process and Movement in Christian Churches*, London: Darton, Longman & Todd.

Roads, J. (2015), 'The Distinctiveness of Quaker Prose, 1650–1699: A Corpus-based Enquiry', PhD thesis, University of Birmingham.

Rowling, J. K. (1999), *Harry Potter and the Prisoner of Azkaban*, London: Bloomsbury.

Schaff, P. (ed.) (1886), *A Select Library of Nicene and Post-Nicene Fathers of the Christian Church: Volume I: The Confessions and Letters of St. Augustin, with a Sketch of his Life and Work*, Edinburgh: T & T Clark.

Scruton, R. (2012), *Our Church: A Personal History of the Church of England*, London: Atlantic Books.

Seeman, M. V. (1983), 'The Unconscious Meaning of Personal Names', *Names* 31(4), pp. 237–44.

Smith, G. (2008), *A Short History of Secularism*, London: I. B. Tauris.

Smith-Bannister, S. (1997), *Names and Naming Patterns in England, 1538–1700*, Oxford: Clarendon Press.

Squires, N. (2011), 'Pope Rails Against Rise of Un-Christian Names', *The Telegraph*. Retrieved 16.12.16, from www.telegraph.co.uk/news/worldnews/the-pope/8251791/Pope-rails-against-rise-of-un-Christian-names.html.

Swatos Jr, W. H. (1998), 'Church–Sect Theory', in *Encyclopedia of Religion and Society*, ed. W. H. Swatos, W. H. Swatos Jr. and P. Kivisto, Walnut Creek, CA: AltaMira Press, pp. 90–3.

The Doctrine Commission of the Church of England (1976), *Christian Believing: The Nature of the Christian Faith and Its Expression in Holy Scripture and Creeds*, London: SPCK.

The Doctrine Commission of the Church of England (1981), *Believing in the Church: The Corporate Nature of Faith*, London: SPCK.

The Guardian (2016), 'Guardian and Observer style guide: C', London. Retrieved 21.6.17, from www.theguardian.com/guardian-observer-style-guide-c.

Thomas, R. (2003), *Counting People In: Changing the Way We Think about Membership and the Church*, London: SPCK.

Thomas, S. (2000), *Your Baby's Baptism in the Anglican Church*, Stowmarket: Kevin Mayhew.

Todd, A. (2005), 'Repertoires or Nodes? Constructing Meanings in Bible-study Groups', *Journal of Applied Linguistics* 2(2), pp. 1288.

Towler, R. and Chamberlain, A. (1973), 'Common Religion', in *A Sociological Yearbook of Religion in Britain*, Vol. 6, ed. M. Hill, London: SCM Press, pp. 1–28.

Troeltsch, E. (1931), *The Social Teaching of the Christian Churches*, Vol. 2, trans. Olive Wyon, London: Allen & Unwin.

UN General Assembly (20 November 1959), 'Declaration of the Rights of the Child', A/RES/1386(XIV). Retrieved 3.2.17, from www.un.org/ga/search/view_doc.asp?symbol=A/RES/1386(XIV),

Village, A. and Francis, L. J. (2009), *The Mind of the Anglican Clergy: Assessing Attitudes and Beliefs in the Church of England*, Lewiston, ME: Edwin Mellen Press.

Weber, M. (1930), *The Protestant Ethic and the Spirit of Capitalism*, trans. Talcott Parsons, with an Introduction by Anthony Giddens, London: Routledge Classics.

Weber, M. et al. (1973), 'Max Weber on Church, Sect, and Mysticism', *Sociological Analysis* 34(2), pp. 140–9.

Welsby, P. A. (1984), *A History of the Church of England, 1945–1980*, Oxford: Oxford University Press.

Wessels, A. (1994), *Europe: Was It Ever Really Christian? The Interaction between Gospel and Culture*, London: SCM Press.

Wilson, S. (1998), *The Means of Naming: A Social and Cultural History of Personal Naming in Western Europe*, London: UCL Press.

Woodhead, L. (2015), 'The Challenges that the New C of E Reports Duck', *Church Times*, 23 January 2015, pp. 14–15.

Woodhead, L. (2016), 'Why "No Religion" is the New Religion'. Retrieved 24.5.17, from www.youtube.com/watch?v=hPLsuW-TCtA.

Woodhead, L. and Catto, R. (eds) (2012), *Religion and Change in Modern Britain*, London: Routledge.

World Council of Churches (1982), *Baptism, Eucharist and Ministry*, Geneva: World Council of Churches.

Wright, D. F. (2005), *What has Infant Baptism Done to Baptism? An Enquiry at the End of Christendom*, Milton Keynes: Paternoster Press.

www.abernook.com (2005), 'To My Godchild', Pinterest. Retrieved 8.2.17, from https://uk.pinterest.com/pin/192388215306457266/.

Wycliffe, J., Tyndale, W., Bosworth, J. and Waring, G. (1888), *The Gothic and Anglo-Saxon Gospels in Parallel Columns with the Versions of Wycliffe and Tyndale; Arranged, with Preface and Notes*, London: Reeves & Turner.

Žižek, S. (1998), 'The Interpassive Subject'. Retrieved 21.6.16, from www.lacan.com/zizek-pompidou.htm.

Index of Names and Subjects